Turning your business into a success mu̶ ̶̶ ̶̶̶̶̶ ̶̶̶̶̶ ̶̶̶̶ for any anyone who wants to create a pipeline of qualified quality leads and increase their sales and profits. Demonstrating Chris' passion for strategy and skills as a master sales coach there are many practical tips and examples. This book shows how targeting the ideal tier 1 client, solving their problem, providing exceptional value, and developing an ongoing authentic relationship rather than the cheesy sales tactics so often promoted to increase sales and profit will produce superior results. Colourfully brought to life with case studies and scenarios, this business book is an easy and entertaining read. Whether you're just starting out or an established business, there are key learnings and a strategic approach to reach significant vertical growth and success.

Dr Liz Isenring
Director of LINC Nutrition & Adjunct Professor,
Bond University

Very interesting approach to sales with social media. I was surprised how much I enjoyed this book. I have had a lot of experience with sales, but I still picked up some good ideas that will help.

Phil Gosschalk, Director, ChildPsych

My advice to the reader is to keep the book handy and re-read it every few months when there is nothing on TV. Each time you read it you get more useful tips.

Les Stock, Director, Worldwide Paramatta

Harasty writes well and his core strategy is sound. The book is a must-read for anyone selling B2B services. I do, however, have to say upfront that some of the strategies will be more useful for people running a business with a sales team.

Sarah McAvoy, Director, Cyberunlocked

The book is worth reading. It is has some useful insights that I haven't read before.

Wayne Dive, Mortgage Broker, REA Group

If you're in B2B sales, you should definitely buy this book. The problem was the tone of the book. It felt like Harasty was bragging about his customer wins. If you can ignore that, well worth the read.

Andrew Hall, CEO, Factory One

Chris Harasty' Success Monster book, was given to me as required reading from my boss. It is different than most other business books. This one has a step-by-step plan of what to do at work. I recommend this book for anyone who has a sales team or is in marketing. This is the type of book that you will want to keep using at work.

Brad Murphy, Senior Account Manager,
Apex Signage

Most of all I have to say that I am lost for words after reading your book. It was a complete surprise for me. A stroke of genius, the way you have interwoven perspective and learning with realism and fiction. The read was easy yet engaging and informative. It teaches how to go about business while living life. Indeed, it is not a one-time read, like most of your reviewers have said but something that needs to be revisited at every turn and twist. It's like an onion with layers to it!

Dr Vasantha Birudavolu,
Viral Marketing Consultant

Turning Your Business into a Success Monster:

The LinkedIn B2B Lead Generation Revolution

Chris Harasty

Dedication

This book is dedicated to Eva Harasty and Bela Harasty, my beloved parents. They were brave enough to leave their war-torn homeland as penniless refugees to build a better life for their family. Although you have both passed, it is now time for me to thank them. This book is for you both.

Table of Contents

Preface

Growing up, I would often hear *scientia potentia est*. This Latin phrase was an obsession for my father. More accurately, the meaning of the phrase was a principle my father believed in so strongly that somehow any topic of conversation inevitably ended with a lecture on this.

Translated literally, it means 'knowledge is power.' The phrase is thought to have originated from Sir Francis Bacon in his work *Meditationes Sacrae* (1597). However, on closer inspection, Bacon mentions a related but slightly different phrase, *ipsa scientia potestas est*, which means 'knowledge itself is power.' The exact phrase was written for the first time by Thomas Hobbes in the legendary work *Leviathan* (1668). Interestingly, a young Hobbes was a secretary to Bacon.

The distinction seems minor, and indeed, the detail would have been lost on a young 10-year boy who desperately wanted to finish his dinner without more Latin. In my young mind, a T-bone steak should be served with pepper sauce, not a Latin lecture. Surprisingly, the distinction is essential, and it holds the key to successful B2B Lead generation, the book's topic. How bizarre is it that my father's dinner lectures turned out to be on the right track and the inspiration for my first book?

Almost 50 years later, I vividly remember how I responded. My father was a strict disciplinarian, while my mother was the heart of the family. My home was not a democracy; survival instincts taught me that I needed to agree with my father early on. The more enthusiastically I agreed, the shorter the lecture. Yet over the years, Dad's Latin proverbs would ring in my head at times of crisis and moments of truth, and the answers to my challenges would appear. So perhaps I was listening, but I didn't know it at the time.

Over the last 20 years, the trend in business-to-business (B2B) commerce has seen significant adverse changes to the business environment. It is becoming increasingly difficult for B2B businesses to survive.

In my sales and business coaching practice, I advise my clients that:

"95% of business problems vanish if you double your sales at a 10% higher margin."

My clients would reply, "Yes, of course, but how?"

After 15 years, I have decided to write a book to answer this question. It turns out that increasing sales while simultaneously growing the profit margin is a challenging endeavor, typically achieved only by the elite. To illustrate this point, I now call this quest "The holy grail of B2B sales."

The **Holy Grail** is a treasure that serves as an important theme in literature. Different traditions describe it as a cup, dish, or stone with miraculous powers that provide eternal youth or sustenance in infinite abundance. It denotes an elusive object or goal sought after for its great significance.

In the B2B context, the holy grail is to create a cold sales and marketing system that automatically and continuously generates an oversupply of interested, warm leads willing to pay a premium for your products or services.

In this system, the salespeople become 'order takers,' and you can double their sales at a 10% higher margin within a few short years. That is what this book is about.

At times, I introduce you to our clients. Anonymity dictates that the names and details are changed to protect confidentiality. Any resemblance to people is purely coincidental, but the principles and the lessons learned are universal and timeless. With the experience of working with more than 3,000 clients over the last 15 years, I have learned that although the business and industry change, the issues remain the same.

I will, at times, explain a few essential elements of coaching psychology theory simply and practically. Most sales and business coaches have little or no qualifications in Psychology and thereby coach with gut instinct rather than an evidence-based playbook. This lack of basic knowledge can be dangerous for some vulnerable clients. You wouldn't let a carpenter operate on your broken leg, yet that happens every day in our industry. Perhaps one day, coaching will become a regulated profession like doctors and psychologists. Until then, some more Latin, *caveat emptor*; let the buyer beware.

Let the treasure hunt begin!

CHAPTER 1

The Blazing Phoenix

B rody is the owner of a small, soon-to-be mid-sized print, signage, and graphic design company called Blaze. I started work with Blaze ten years ago when Kevin and Chloe were the owners. Kevin and Chloe met in design school, bonded over color theory, and married in a print factory. Chloe was of German descent, and she approached life with a terse directness that left people wondering what had just transpired in their interaction. Kevin, however, saw life through a black and white lens and was remarkedly adept at avoiding responsibility.

Kevin and Chloe shared a passion for arguing. They argued in front of their staff, customers, and suppliers. For most couples, arguing unsettles the relationship and, if left unchecked, starts a sad decline, but this was not the case for Kevin and Chloe. Perhaps arguing stirred the passion in their marriage and formed the glue that bonded them.

Blaze thrived in the early stages.

Chloe was a great designer, perhaps in the top 5% of her peers. Kevin, not quite as talented, was firmly at the other end of the spectrum. Understanding his limitations, Kevin decided to move to the adjacent role of printing and factory management. This shift turned out to be a clever strategic move. Offering a one-stop shop for print and design provided a good competitive advantage for the business. The design was great, and the price was below the market rate, so inevitably the business grew.

Like many small businesses, Kevin and Chloe had stumbled onto a formula that worked. Driven more by luck than strategic business planning, the company grew. Over the years, it built a tremendous portfolio of work and a client list of impressive brands and large corporations.

Life was good – until one day it wasn't.

Kevin reached out to my sales coaching practice after three lean years. Blaze had been on a slow downward spiral since the market entry of low-cost suppliers from India and China in the early 1990s. With low-cost labor, the Indian outsourcer sold at 30% of the market rate, causing a tectonic shift in the marketplace. Unfortunately, Blaze was devoid of answers to this enormous issue.

Perhaps the quality was not quite as good as the local supplier but saving 70% of the cost was too tempting for many customers. The vast price difference forced customers to ask: *How much difference does the extra quality make? Is it really worth paying thrice as much for the same thing?*

Many businesses surviving on good fortune rather than rigorous business planning did not survive in this harsh business environment.

After detailed conversations with Kevin and Chloe, I assisted them in doubling their business twice over the next five years until the next major crisis emerged. By now, with many miles on the clock, Kevin and Chloe were exhausted from the relentless stress and yearned for a change.

Promising them a forum for peace in our fortnightly meetings, my skills were insufficient to appease the warring couple. Perhaps Henry Kissinger was better suited to this challenge than the Master Coach.

An aging Kevin decided that health, not wealth, was the priority and that a sea-change was required. Ironically, the sea-change was not located next to the beach; it was an inland acreage that beckoned the family. As luck would have it, Kevin found a buyer for the business, and Brody inherited the chaotic mess with great potential.

Kevin and Chloe stayed with the business to ease the transition, and much to my surprise, I was re-engaged to fuel the growth.

Blaze was reborn from the ashes.

Brody came from the same industry with a background in production management with a much larger organization. The day-to-day chaos was slowly replaced with structure, process, and planning. This restructure was fortunate for me, as the Master Coach is supremely effective in a structured business hungry to grow.

The myth of the phoenix bird represents immortality, rebirth, and life after death. In ancient Greek mythology, it is associated with the Sun God. The Greeks believed that every dawn, the Sun God would stop his chariot to listen to the birds sing a beautiful song while he bathed in the water. Only one phoenix lived at a time; when the bird sensed its death was nigh, it would build a nest and set it on fire. The bird consumed by the flames was subsequently reborn. So it was for Blaze, now led by Brody, the Sun God.

The 2004 film, *The Flight of the Phoenix,* is a remake of the original 1965 classic. It stars Dennis Quaid, Giovanni Ribisi, and

Miranda Otto. The plot is simple; the plane encounters a major dust storm flying over the desert and is forced to crash land in the Gobi Desert. Danger abounds in the hot desert, and with water in short supply, survival seems bleak. Personalities grind, and tempers flare as death seems imminent.

A passenger, Elliot, suggests that it may be possible to re-build the plane. Eventually, the group agrees, and work begins. Later, it is revealed that Elliot builds model planes, not real ones. Emotions run high, but the recriminations recede as bandits attack the group. The plane takes off, narrowly escaping the bandits—good triumphs over evil.

The film was a box office failure, but it was a decent movie with good acting, picturesque scenery, and photography. For me, the movie shines with its core metaphor; rarely does positive change follow a structured, intentional path. If humans were sensible, this might have been the case.

Often success breeds complacency, and eventually, that starts the fire. The rebirth of Blaze allowed me to revisit the benefits of chasing the holy grail, my work passion, and my obsession. Blaze had excellent prospects, but we needed to find the holy grail to reach its potential.

This book is about how we found the holy grail for Blaze and created a golden prize for the business. From a position that even I thought was utterly impossible, we built a sales and marketing system that made cold marketing as easy as a fire blazon hot knife slicing through butter.

In our first fortnightly session, Brody asked, "Chris, you know we have many problems. Where do we start?"

"Good question. We need to learn how to grow sales at a higher margin," I replied.

"Wow, that sounds like a big challenge. How on earth do we do that?"

"Next fortnight, we start by looking at the sales function in the business. I will send you an email with the PDF copy of lecture one. Will you have time to read it by our next session?"

"Yes," Brody said.

Brody had taken the first step. Instead of watching the football on TV with an ice-cold beer, Brody snuck into the study and gleefully skimmed lecture one.

The journey had begun.

The Fill-the-Pipe Program

Lecture 1: The Overview

"95% of business problems are solved with more sales at a higher margin."

Chris Harasty

Research into the B2B sector reveals that new customer acquisition is one of the top priorities for small to medium-sized businesses. The main obstacle to sales growth is generating an oversupply of interested, warm leads. The fill-the-pipe lecture series describes a simple and effective process for B2B sales and marketing professionals to solve this issue. We present an overview of the program in this lecture.

The Purpose of the Fill-the-Pipe Program

- According to the U.S. Bureau of Labor Statistics (BLS), the percentage of businesses that fail is:
  - 20% in the first two years
  - 45% within five years
  - 65% within ten years
  - Only 25% survive more than fifteen years.
  - The failure tends to be because of a lack of strategic planning and understanding that as the business grows the planning process needs to change.
- As a rule of thumb for small to medium-sized businesses:
  - *Most business problems are solved with more sales at a higher margin*
- The purpose of the fill-the-pipe program is to explain in detail how to increase sales at a higher margin.
- The ambitious target we suggest for the participant is to select a goal that may seem unattainable. We suggest the following goal:
  - Double sales at a higher margin within 12-24 months

Who is the Program Designed for?

- The program is designed specifically for businesses that sell B2B products and services o   It is suitable for individuals with the following work responsibilities:

- Sales Professionals
- Sales Managers
- Sales Directors
- Marketing Professionals
- Marketing Managers
- Marketing Directors
- Owners and Directors responsible for sales growth

Why is the Program Required?

- The traditional B2B sales and marketing methods are becoming less effective each year. The recent industry trends suggest a rapid decline in the effectiveness of the traditional techniques, making them unviable within the next five years.
- The advent of social media promises an amazing renaissance in B2B sales and marketing. The potential to communicate with a global audience and deliver a marketing campaign that goes "*viral*" promises a revolution in lead generation.
- The reality is more mundane. Standard social media practices have focused on B2C communication, and these practices are less effective in the B2B marketplace.
- The fill-the-pipe program bridges the gap between the desire to leverage social media for B2B marketing and the practical methods of communication

with a B2B audience that is effective for lead generation. It explains new social media strategies and a simple process designed explicitly for the B2B marketplace. The new methods are effective and easy to implement.

The Traditional B2B 1% Rule

- For traditional B2B cold sales and marketing campaigns, a 1% response is typical.
  - o Sales function (cold calling): typically generates a 1% response rate
  - o Marketing function (cold direct email): typically generates a 1% response rate
- The 1% response rate includes responses that are: positive, neutral, and negative. The positive response rate is usually significantly lower than 1%.
- Therefore, for traditional cold sales and marketing methods to produce a good result, a high volume of activity is required to generate new sales.
- Cold calling with a positive response rate of < 1% is often soul-destroying for many salespeople. The continual rejection is difficult to withstand, and many salespeople give up, defeated.

Why Is Cold Calling So Difficult?

- *Salespeople have an aversion to cold calling.* Salespeople usually hate making cold calls due to continual rejection, and they tend to avoid cold calling and often don't do enough calls to get a result.

- *It is challenging to contact decision-makers*, and gate-keepers and voice mail systems have been established to block callers from reaching the senior decision-makers.
- *Flood of Bad Overseas Calls.* The US market is full of poor-quality cold calls from overseas call centres where the agents struggle to speak English.
- *Low Conversion Rate.* The effort required to get an appointment is high, and the prospects' desire to purchase is often low.

Why are Cold Email Campaigns Becoming Less Effective?

- A cold email is an unsolicited email sent without prior contact with the target. The distinction between a cold email and spam is somewhat arbitrary.
- Marketers argue that cold email is not considered spam if it is an adequately personalized message. The message needs to be specifically tailored for the individual to start a business conversation. In contrast, spam promotes a product or a service to a mass audience with a generic message.
- Most recipients tend to regard a cold email as spam unless they are currently interested in it. In other words, the email subject line needs to align with a current business priority for the recipient to be tempted to open the email.
- Spam filters block a high percentage of cold emails, and research shows that individuals tend to remove over 85% of cold emails before reading.

Social Media

- Large social media platforms like Facebook, Instagram, and Twitter are designed for public and B2C communication. They can be used for B2B marketing; however, the campaigns tend to be expensive. They are not effective because the targeting functionality of the platforms is not suited to B2B segmentation.
- LinkedIn is emerging as the best social media platform for the B2B sector. However, there are some challenges, including:
  - o LinkedIn was created as a professional networking tool, not a sales tool.
  - o LinkedIn aggressively protects its members against standard cold marketing methods, and members using cold marketing methods will have their accounts restricted by LinkedIn.
- The fill-the-pipe program presents a new lead generation method that leverages LinkedIn, complies with the LinkedIn restrictions, and delivers a continuous stream of warm leads.

The Holy Grail of B2B Sales and Marketing

- The **Holy Grail** is powerful mythology in ancient history and literature, and it represents a lost treasure with magical powers that bestows eternal youth or vast wealth. As a metaphor in literature, it signifies a treacherous quest to locate the magical object that solves the catastrophe with mystical powers.

- In the B2B context, the holy grail is to create a cold sales and marketing system that automatically and continuously generates an oversupply of warm leads willing to pay a premium for your products or services. In this system, the salespeople become 'order takers,' and you can double sales within a few short years.
- The lecture series explains how to create your own *Holy Grail* of B2B lead generation system leveraging social media.

The Three Steps to the Holy Grail

- The three steps to create the Holy Grail system includes:
  - Strategic Planning
  - The 1-a-week prospecting approach
  - Over delivery

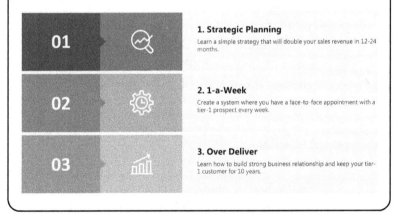

1. Strategic Planning
Learn a simple strategy that will double your sales revenue in 12-24 months.

2. 1-a-Week
Create a system where you have a face-to-face appointment with a tier-1 prospect every week.

3. Over Deliver
Learn how to build strong business relationship and keep your tier-1 customer for 10 years.

- Before discussing the three steps described above, we need to deal with the core prerequisites. The basic hygiene of the business is discussed in the following three lectures.

Summary of Key Points

- The traditional B2B sales and marketing methods are becoming less effective each year. The recent industry trends suggest a rapid decline in the effectiveness of the traditional techniques making these methods unviable within the next five years.
- The Traditional B2B 1% Rule states that cold sales and marketing campaigns typically generate a 1% response rate.
- The B2B holy grail is to create a cold sales and marketing system that automatically and continuously generates an oversupply of warm leads willing to pay a premium for your products or services.
- LinkedIn has emerged as the *Best Performing Social Media Platform* for B2B sales and marketing.
- Members must abide by the LinkedIn Code of Conduct.

Suggested Reading

https://www.b2bmarketing.net/

Charged with excitement, Brody couldn't sleep. He felt compelled to turn the page and start reading the next chapter.

CHAPTER 2

Can You Catch a Unicorn?

Mason Bell and Jack Allen were friends. They battled on the squash court every Wednesday night after work. Wednesday was chosen deliberately not to interfere with the magical Super Bowl Sunday night. NFL was a great vicarious theatre for competition and a metaphor for life. At an age when the body started to decline, they were still fierce competitors on the court, and they both hated losing as losing bestowed the privilege of buying drinks after the game, nullifying the benefit of the exercise. Notice I didn't mention dinner; alcohol would amply suffice after the 'virtual' world championship semi-finals. Without the TV crew and pundits, no one kept score apart from the two gladiators.

Jack seemed like an unusual choice of a friend for Mason. Jack was never the sporting hero at school, and he excelled in music and drama and walked the stage each year to collect his academic prize. With college predestined at birth by his doting parents, Jack followed the chosen path with little resistance. In the narrow college cloisters, Jack's achievements came effortlessly using his natural academic strength.

Life changed dramatically after college. Leaving behind the academic environment, Jack took a leap of faith and started his own business providing web development. Strategically calculating that his future career should ride the wave of the latest never-ending revolution, Jack hung up his shingle and expected to be swamped with clients begging to be saved. Perhaps, this was a bit naïve.

Mason was the dominant alpha male and star of the school football team; he was cool at school. Twenty years had still not reduced his competitive killer instinct, and natural strength endowed Mason with unyielding confidence, which translated into his business life. Surrounded by four women at home, Mason's wife Suzy gave birth to a small women's club. Dolls and Disney princesses were no longer foreign to Mason, who longed for his weekly dose of Wednesday testosterone.

Mason had accidentally stumbled into the recruiting industry. Without the need to waste time in college, Mason was 'picked up' by a small sales recruiting company owned by Joe Stone. As the first trainee with no other associates, Mason was lucky to be personally trained by the owner. Mason seemed to be naturally gifted in his business life, to his surprise. As an alpha male, Mason enjoyed the odious task of cold calling, and it reminded him of chasing girls at school. The word no was never a deterrent; it merely presented a more exciting conversion challenge. With this innate positive attitude, Mason excelled in his role from day one. Mason was officially a unicorn after his first month at his job.

Mason had embraced wireless headphones well before Bluetooth propelled the device to supermarket shelves. Wireless headphones enabled freedom in a dull-tethered working day. Mason was different; he was born with a skill possessed by few and harnessed by only a handful of unicorns. Unicorns, in the business world, have a much sought-after magical power. They enjoy the odious task of cold calling.

Fate continued to smile on Mason.

Joe, the owner of the sales recruiting business, was experiencing a purple patch in his life. The business was the best it had ever been, with Mason outperforming even the highest expectations. Joe was in love. How could life be any better? Scarred by an ugly divorce, Joe had gained 20 pounds and sworn never to be involved in another relationship. Having lost half his assets, Joe was acidly skeptical about life. Until one rainy day, rushing to the car park, Joe lent his umbrella to Naomi. In less than 100 yards to where Joe had parked his car, he was completely drenched in water and love. Heart pounding, Joe strategically allowed Naomi to keep the umbrella and return it at her leisure. Little did he know, Joe's peculiar custom of engraving his name and mobile number on his possessions transformed his life.

Two weeks later, over dinner, Joe was brimming with anticipation and boyhood excitement. Although Naomi was ten years younger than Joe, they connected in a magical conversation that lasted all night and much of the following morning. Interrupted by the sounds of the city waking up, Joe somehow erased the painful memory of his ex-wife and decided that he would marry Naomi. After all, life was short, and there was no time to waste. Joe was undoubtedly correct in that department.

A week before the blessed wedding, Joe suffered a massive stroke and died instantly. Naomi was inconsolable, and Joe's shattered parents organized a funeral reception in the same venue where the wedding reception was planned. Mason seized the opportunity, usurped the business in the ensuing chaos, and renamed it *Mason Bell Recruiting*. More than half the clients left, but the remaining half was enough to catapult Mason into his first business venture. In the cycle of life, vultures pick the carcass with no regrets.

Less than a mile north of Mason's office, Jack Kent watched the traffic dribble past from his almost comfortable office chair, occupied in his thoughts. Instead of working efficiently, Jack mastered the intricacies of procrastination. Everything was in place at his office: the pencils were sharp, the desk was tidy, and the list was meticulously prepared. Jack could focus on anything but what he was supposed to do.

Although the squash contenders were leading separate lives, fate had other plans for them. One day, Jack reached out to Mason for help. Naturally, the alpha male was delighted to help his friend and provide advice. In a flash of rare insight, Mason understood that his natural skill was challenging to replicate. After all, there is only one quarterback on the field. Mason correctly advised Jack not to try cold calling but to contact an expert professional to create a proper sales function in the business. In Mason's opinion, Jack was better to focus on the technical web development and get a sales partner or develop a system to perform the sales function; good advice from the new business owner. Jack hurried home and spent a few hours Googling until he finally found our program.

After a fortnight of internet research and several zoom interviews, Jack engaged in our LinkedIn B2B Lead Generation free trial program. Demanding an immediate start and knowing that Jack was an intellectual, the PDF of our first lecture was in his inbox before we finished our call.

Jack devoured the information and sent me a list of questions after midnight. The answers were much more straightforward than Jack expected, but that is the lesson he needed to learn. Every client is different, and my job is to help them learn how to overcome their business challenges. In most cases, the challenges are related to their weaknesses, which makes the process difficult and exciting – for me. Very few people want to work on their weaknesses because it is much more fun to stay in your comfort zone and play to your strengths. Many businesses tend to struggle with their sales and marketing functions because they don't start at the beginning and master the basics.

The Fill-the-Pipe Program

Lecture 2: The Sales Function

"The sales and delivery functions are considered equally important in business, but in my opinion, sales are slightly more important because, without sales, nothing happens."

Chris Harasty

The sales function refers to the activities of selling products or services to customers and prospects. A sale is a transaction between two parties where the buyer receives products or services in exchange for money. Legally, it is represented by a contract between the buyer and the seller at a specified price.

The Importance of the Sales Function

- What is the most crucial part of a business that is critical for its survival? Is it the staff or the customer service, or the product?

- For a business to succeed, each department needs to perform well and work together to generate customer value and satisfy customer requirements effectively and efficiently.
- All parts of the business are equally important, but one department is first among equals: sales. The sales department is the essential part of a business because nothing happens until a sale is closed, and the business will not exist if there are no sales.

The Sales Function

- The sales function is involved in many parts of the business. Some of the critical elements are listed below:
  - Customer conversion
  - Customer retention
  - Revenue forecasts
  - New product development
  - Business growth
- **Customer Conversion** – occurs when customers purchase from the business generating sales revenue. The sales department is responsible for the conversion, and it should be tracked to report the customer conversion rate metric.
- **Customer Retention** – is focused on building a solid business relationship with existing customers to encourage repeat purchases. Customer retention strategies are focused on:
  - Creating strong customer relationships
  - Customer service

- o Quality of products and services
- o Loyalty programs

The sales department is responsible for implementing customer retention strategies.

- **Revenue forecasts** – the efficient allocation of resources is required for the business to survive and generate profit. Accurate sales forecasts are an essential factor in planning and controlling business efficiency.
- **New product development** – depends on salespeople to deeply understand customer requirements and provide feedback to the marketing and product development team. New products and services are unlikely to succeed without this direct customer feedback.
- **Business growth** – occurs when the sales team increases the business's annual revenue, and revenue growth can generate more transactions with existing customers or new customer acquisitions.

The New Customer Acquisition Paradox

- The new customer acquisition paradox is a new term we devised to represent the perennial challenge of business growth. New customer acquisition tends to be the most significant factor that can increase sales revenue, but it also tends to be the most difficult to achieve. The paradox is that the best growth method is the most difficult to achieve.

In many businesses, the principal factor that increases sales revenue is new customer acquisition, and the most important factor that enables new customer acquisition is lead generation. Therefore, an oversupply of new warm leads is the critical success factor required to generate sales growth with new customer acquisitions.

The Sales and Marketing Process

The end-to-end sales and marketing process includes seven steps.

1. **Prospecting**

   Prospecting involves identifying and qualifying prospects. Qualification determines whether the prospect has a legitimate requirement that the business can solve and whether the prospect has a sufficient budget to purchase the product or service.

2. **Preparation**

   Preparation involves planning for the initial discussion with the prospect. The salesperson will need to research the prospect to understand their business. Usually, the prospect's website has the required information.

3. **Cold Reach Out**

   The reach out is the initial cold approach to the prospect. Often this is the most challenging step in the sales and marketing process as there is a high percentage of rejection. An effective cold reach process is explained later in this lecture series.

4. **The Sales Meeting**

   The sales meeting is a face-to-face conversation between the salesperson and the prospect. The sales meeting conversation has a distinct process that involves four stages:

   o Rapport
   o Discovery
   o Conviction
   o Commitment

   This process is described in detail in a separate sales training program.

- **The Sales Approach** is designed to quickly engage the prospect in the sales conversation. There are three main options:

   o **Gift Approach** – To build rapport, the salesperson gives the prospect a gift at the beginning of the meeting. It could be a small gift like a pen or USB memory stick. This approach is not recommended.

   o **Question approach** – To understand the prospect's requirements, the salesperson asks probing questions.

   o **Product trial approach** – To show that the salesperson is confident in their product, they give the prospect a product sample to review.

5. **The Sales Proposal and Presentation**

   After understanding the prospect's requirements, the salesperson creates a solution and documents it in a proposal and a presentation. The documents demonstrate how the solution addresses the prospect's needs.

6. **Handling Objections**

   The objection handling stage is an integral part of the sales process. Objections signal the salesperson should focus on the prospect's issues. Successful salespeople can overcome objections with scripts and empathetic negotiation.

7. **Closing the Sale**

   The close involves identifying closing signals that indicate that a decision is imminent. There are many different approaches to closing a sale, and some of the techniques involve:

   o **Puppy dog close** – the salesperson provides the prospect the product on trial for a week, and if they like it, you send an invoice. Otherwise, they can return the product.

   o **Assumptive close** – the salesperson assumes the prospect wants to purchase and offers the prospect a choice: "How do you want to pay for it? With credit card or direct bank deposit?"

   o **Bonus close** – the salesperson offers extra value to reach an agreement with the buyer, and it could be an additional free product or a discount.

   o **Limited time close** – the salesperson advises the prospect that the offer expires after a short period. For example, the price may be increased 10% next month.

   o **No closing technique** – we do not recommend using a closing technique, and it may be interpreted as a 'salesy' technique.

8. **After-Sale**
   The after-sale step is building a long-term, strong business relationship with the customer to encourage repeat business.

Summary of Key Points

- All parts of the business are equally important. Still, the sales department is the most critical part of a business because nothing happens until a sale is closed, and the business will not exist if there are no sales.
- New customer acquisition is critical for the survival of a business.
- The new customer acquisition paradox states that new customer acquisition tends to be the most prominent factor in increasing sales revenue. Still, it also tends to be the most difficult to achieve.

Suggested Reading

The Ultimate Sales Machine *by Chet Holmes*

SPIN Selling *by Neil Rackham*

Selling to Big Companies *by Jill Konrath*

Solution Selling *by Michael T. Bosworth*

The New Strategic Selling *by Robert B. Miller & Stephen E. Heiman*

The Challenger Sale *by Matthew Dixon & Brent Adamson*

Predictable Revenue *by Aaron Ross & Marylou Tyler*

Jack was a fast learner, but he implemented at a snail's pace. Jack understood theoretical concepts by just reading the PDF once. This skill was rare; most people need to read the information, discuss it with an expert, and only learn when they start implementing and seeing results. Learning through action is well-suited to adults; it is called experiential learning. Experiential learning is what we use in our practice, and it works great for our clients.

Learning is only the first step, and it is useless unless the client implements something. Often, even a tiny partial implementation provides a good result. In this department, Jack needed work, and I pondered how to crack this tough nut.

While driving, I had heard on the radio that the pistachio wallop walnut was the hardest nut in the world. Notburga Gierlinger, a biophysicist at the University of Natural Resources and Life Sciences in Vienna, discussed the intricacies of the famous pistachio. Notburga and her colleagues discovered the secret of why the shells are so strong. The nuts are covered in a microscopic structure of interlocking cells so tightly bound that they never let go of each other. The material is strong enough that it might one day be used for shock-absorbing items such as safety helmets. Naomi Nakayama, a bioengineer at Imperial College London who was not involved in the work, said, *"These tissues achieve a holy grail of materials science."* How strange, Nakayama's first name was Naomi, and she mentioned the holy grail. What a bizarre coincidence indeed.

While I was pondering this absurd digression, the answer came to me. Jack is competitive, and his friend Mason is a unicorn. Perhaps if I structure the task as a squash game against Mason, that may be enough motivation to shock Jack into some action. All I wanted was for some action to happen. As long as we started, I knew we would be successful. In technical coaching psychology terms, Jack was stuck in the second stage of the transtheoretical model of change: 'contemplation,' two steps before 'action.' I had discovered what I thought was a defibrillator that could work to jolt Jack into action, but I wasn't sure if it would deliver enough charge (motivation) to work. Below the required threshold, nothing happens. It turns out that I had found the 'hot spot,' and the shock was more than enough to hurtle Jack into motion. The potential of beating the alpha male friend with a more innovative strategy was far more potent than the fear of failure.

Action is essential; what is also important is that we need to head in the right direction.

Before we can customize a sales process for Jack, he needs to learn the steps in the standard sales procedure.

In almost every coaching engagement, building the client's confidence is as important as building their new business skills or formulating a new strategy. The technical term in coaching psychology is 'self-efficacy,' It plays a vital role in goal attainment. Often self-efficacy can be quite different or counter-intuitive to what non-professionally qualified coaches believe. Unfortunately, many common-sense coaching interventions blindly followed by unqualified coaches have undesirable effects. Mercifully, most clients are not discerning, and the coach survives to live another day.

Al Pacino portrays an aging NFL coach in the prodigious movie *Any Given Sunday*. In a rousing speech before the game, Pacino delivers a motivational team talk moments before they march out of the dressing room to do battle. Even though I have watched the video a hundred times, I get goosebumps listening to the powerful monologue every time. Pacino's performance is magnificent.

My Al Pacino monologue was not powerful eloquent words; it was merely a quick sharp poke with a snooker cue. Jack's ball was in motion, and now, I wondered if it was headed for the pocket.

Did Jack have the confidence and resilience to overcome the next impending challenge, or would the alpha male win again?

For Jack, although he didn't know it yet, the transformation was about to start faster than expected. Whether Jack grasped the baton will be determined by the openness of his personality. I was confident that Jack would prevail, but I didn't know how much suffering it would take for him to reach out for the baton of change.

CHAPTER 3

The Revolution

In October 1956, a group of Hungarian university students gathered to protest the brutal Government of Mátyás Rákosi. Rákosi ruled the country with brutal torture, mass imprisonment, and targeted assassination. Rákosi sent thousands of Hungarian people to their deaths to maintain his hold on power.

Predictably, Rákosi's economic policies were not enlightened; the Government's collectivization policy destroyed the economy, and the people were suffering in poverty. Plagued with impoverishment and brutal oppression, the people craved change. After a decade of Rákosi oppression, university students decided to rebel.

A group of students decided that the best way to communicate the public demand was to take control of the Hungarian Radio building and broadcast their demands. Had it been 50 years later, the students would have chosen social media as their protest vehicle; it certainly would have been a safer choice.

Rákosi hadn't yet embraced the benefits of free speech and political debate. The students were detained and shot. The revolution lasted less than three weeks before brutal suppression recaptured the people. With the Government's attention diverted, my parents saw an opportunity; sick of the terror and violence, they wanted a change. Rather than protest against an immovable power, they fled. Under a dark moonless night, my parents crossed the loosely guarded Austrian border with bullets whistling above their heads. Leaving behind their family and possessions, they left the country because they wanted more, and they were brave enough to take advantage of the opportunity.

How does one come to take such a decision? What motivates people to take radical action and risk their lives for change? Is the new place going to be any better? How do you survive in a new country not knowing how to speak the language?

Language is the cornerstone of communication, understanding people, and relationships. Language enables individuals to formulate thoughts, create new ideas and solve problems. Language is the common fabric of how people experience events and make sense of the world.

Social media is littered with a strange new language, and it promises hope in marketing nirvana. Blogs, posts, LOL; what does it all mean? Perhaps the questions are always the same, and the only difference is their timing.

Leadership development and coaching psychology share a common interest in ambiguity. People experiencing adversity are thrust into an environment that fosters ambiguity and, at times, danger. People tend to be 'meaning-making' machines; they spontaneously evaluate situations and attempt to derive meaning from events. Even when random events occur, and no meaning should be attributed, the mind creates a narrative to fill the vacuum. Often, the narrative may be dysfunctional and hinder progress.

Ambiguity drives stress because the next step is unclear, and the consequences of failure may be high. At the moment, you may feel apprehension and uncertainty, which is normal. Traditional marketing methods are no longer effective and urgently require a solution. We are only at the start of the journey, and the next step is uncertain. Additionally, you may be skeptical that a viable solution will be revealed in the book.

It turns out that functionally dealing with stress and ambiguity is critical to goal attainment and success. Controlling the adverse effects of stress helps decision-making – notice that I did not say eliminating stress. In a famous experiment in 1908, Yerkes and Dodson discovered a relationship between stress and performance. Stress improves performance up to a point, and then it drops significantly.

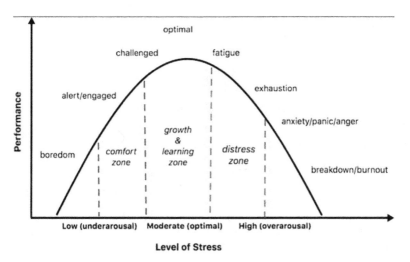

To ensure that a stressed person functions below the turning point, there are two main categories of strategies that are very effective and used by psychologists around the world:

- Problem-focused
- Emotion-focused

Both types of strategies need to be used together to reduce stress.

Emotion-focused coping strategies reduce negative emotions such as fear, anxiety, and depression. Emotion-focused strategies are very effective, but they only treat the symptom, not the root cause. You can think of such strategies as an over-the-counter pain reliever, and Panadol relieves that pain for a few hours, but the pain returns until the root cause is addressed.

Emotion-focused coping strategies may seem pointless, but they are essential. It may take months to implement a solution, so Panadol helps reduce the pain and allows better decision-making. Without Panadol, poor decision-making tends to prolong the suffering needlessly.

The Panadol I recommend is progressive muscle relaxation, a simple process where the person tenses a group of muscles as they breathe in and then relaxes them. Each muscle group in the body is relaxed one at a time. The techniques work because you do not feel stressed when the body is relaxed.

There are many relaxation apps to choose from for people with smartphones, and many of them will be helpful. I use the Calm app narrated by Tamara Levitt. The Calm app has more than 1 million subscribers, and it has developed a near-cult following. Remember, any relaxation app will do the job, but nothing will happen if you do not use it when stressed.

On the other hand, problem-focused coping strategies focus on resolving the root cause of the stress. The effort is aimed at managing or altering the problems causing the stress. The steps to resolve the leading cause include:

1. Define the problem
2. Generate solution options
3. Evaluate the alternatives
4. Develop detailed action plans
5. Identify skill gaps and the resources required

6. Select the best action plan
7. Implement the action plan
8. Modify the plan to stay on track
9. Persist in the journey until successful

Although this seems like a long slow process, the benefits accrue rapidly. As soon as the individual develops a reasonable plan that seems like it may succeed, an element of hope appears, and perhaps half of the stress disappears. The problem-focused version of Panadol is simply to continue reading.

The Fill-the-Pipe Program

Lecture 3: Prospecting & Lead Generation

Social media promise a revolution in B2B marketing, yet over 60% of campaigns are not considered successful. The revolution needs to be in thinking and social media is merely the delivery vehicle.

By Chris Harasty

As we discussed in lecture 1, new customer acquisition is a top priority for marketers. In a 2020 survey, 73% of respondents named new customer acquisition as a key outcome for the upcoming year. For most small to medium sized businesses, the main obstacle to sales growth is generating an oversupply of interested warm leads. Perhaps the most difficult part of the sales process is booking the face-to-face appointment. This lecture explains why lead generation is so difficult and provides an overview of new prospecting methods.

The B2B 1% Rule

- Recall the B2B 1% Rule. For traditional B2B cold sales and marketing campaigns a 1% response is a typical outcome.
  - o Sales Function - Cold calling → 1% response rate
  - o Marketing Function - Cold direct email → 1% response rate
- The 1% response rate includes response that are: positive, neutral, and negative. The positive response rate is usually significantly lower than 1%. Therefore, for traditional cold sales and marketing methods to produce a result, a high volume of activity is required to generate new sales.
- Social media promises to revolutionize B2B marketing with viral marketing campaigns and the power of precise targeting.

Prospecting and Lead Generation

1. Lead generation is a marketing process where the attention and interest of potential customers (prospects) is aroused sufficiently that they are open to engage in a conversation with the marketer. High quality information (content) about the business's products and services is the key driver that generates the interest and starts the conversation.
- Prospecting and lead generation are essential to the success of any organization. Unfortunately, many salespeople view the process as time-consuming,

tedious, and only engage in the bare minimum effort.

- By changing the salesperson's perspective of prospecting and engaging in meaningful and enjoyable activities, the business will benefit from an increase in warm leads.
- Most salespeople understand that prospecting is important to be able to achieve their sales budget, however it is often replaced with less odious. Prospecting needs to become a priority for the sales team.
- For prospecting to be effective it needs to be performed with the following 3 factors:
  - o Professional manner
  - o Preparation
  - o Scheduled (as a daily activity)
- **Scheduling**: Choose a time for prospecting and keep to the schedule. Professional salespeople tend to schedule prospecting early in the morning and do not let any other activities to interrupt their prospecting time.
- **Preparation**: Salespeople should prepare scripts but need to be flexible in their conversations.
- **Professionalism**: Salespeople need to behave in a professional manner during the entire sales process.

Different Prospecting Methods

- There are numerous prospecting methods available. While salespeople may choose multiple methods of prospecting, it is important to focus on methods that the target prospects respond to more favorably.

- Prospecting methods that are commonly used include:
  o Cold calling

  o Referrals

  o Content marketing

  o Email marketing

  o Networking

  o Seminars

  o Social Media

  o Webinars

  o Advertising

Cold Calling

- Cold calling has become increasingly difficult over the last decade. Do not expect to close a sale with a cold call. While it may happen, the purpose is to connect with the prospect.
- Cold calling campaigns requires extensive preparation and strategic planning. The planning should focus on understanding the prospect's requirements and how the value proposition provides a solution.
- The cold call includes 4 steps:
  1. Introducing yourself and your company

  2. Questioning the prospects about their needs

  3. Educating the prospect about how you can meet needs

4. Ask for the face-to-face sales appointment

Why Cold Calling So Difficult

- Salespeople have an aversion to Cold Calling. Salespeople usually hate making cold calls due to the continual rejection. They tend to avoid cold calling and often don't do enough calls to get a result.
- It is difficult to contact decision makers. Gatekeepers and voice mail systems have been established to block callers to be able to contact the senior decision makers.
- Flood of Bad Overseas Calls. The US market is full of poor-quality cold calls from overseas call centers where the agents struggle to speak English.
- Low Conversion Rate. The effort to get an appointment is high and the prospects desire to purchase is often low.

Direct Mail

- Direct mail is a familiar marketing method that uses physical mail, making it simple and affordable. The effectiveness of direct mail requires choosing the mailing list carefully. The list of prospects should be based on the ideal customer profile.
- The marketing collateral needs to specifically target the ideal customer profile. Direct mail campaigns tend to be more effective when there is a call to action, such as a special offer.
- The direct mail collateral can be educational or creative. It should be tested on a sample of the list.

Fine-tuning the collateral and target can increase the performance of the campaign significantly.

Trade Shows

- A trade show is a convenient venue for meeting new prospects. Trade shows are typically crowded and filled with competition. The steps below can help maximize the benefit of attending a trade show:
- Plan in advance: The planning includes finding the best booth space and choosing how to brand the space. The booth should be attended by enthusiastic and energetic staff to handle enquiries.
- Create goals: Set goals for the trade show to keep staff focused. For example, it may be useful to measure the number of prospects that want to meet after the trade show.
- Personal Invitations: Personal invitations are an effective way to strengthen existing customer relationships.
- Follow up: Attending a trade show is expensive. In order to extract the most value from the investment, it is important to implement a reliable follow up process after the trade show.

Networking

- Face-to-face networking is often not an effective method of prospecting. Networking requires time to build relationships. The process is slow, and often does not yield a good return on investment.

New Marketing Methods

- As technology changes, so do the marketing methods used. Some newer marketing methods, such as:
  o Search engine marketing
  o Social media
  o Webinars

have become common prospecting methods in business.

- When the newer marketing methods are combined with the traditional methods, interesting and effective new campaigns emerge.
- Social media is now commonplace in the modern world, and it is rapidly growing as the first-choice method of advertising.
- There are different methods of advertising used in social media:
  o Advertise promotions directly to followers
  o Placing ads on the social media platforms
- Advertising on social media can be expensive. Campaigns need to me measured and the parameters need to be tuned to extract optimal campaign performance.
- B2B Linkedin marketing will be discussed more fully in future lectures.
- Webinars are an effective tool that you can be used to generate new leads and demonstrate expertise. Webinars require a great deal of work and preparation, but they are often worth the effort.
- Webinar Promotion involves:

1. Create a webinar with a title that is likely to be searched by prospective customers.

2. Choose a webinar software platform like zoom or WebEx.

3. Develop a landing page for registration – (for example, eventbrite.com)

4. Advertise the webinar. Use social media, ads, blogs, and newsletters.

- The webinar needs to be prepared well in advance and executed flawlessly. A well-executed webinar needs to be rehearsed many times. Additionally, the technology should be tested beforehand to ensure that there are no nasty surprises.

Assess The ROI

- As with all projects it is imperative to keep track of the return on investment (ROI). The basic ROI calculation is:

(Investment Gain – Cost of investment) / Cost of investment

Summary of Key Points

- Prospecting and lead generation are essential to the success of any organization. Unfortunately, many salespeople view the process as time-consuming, tedious, and only engage in the bare minimum effort.

- Social media promises to revolutionize B2B marketing with viral marketing campaigns and the power of precise targeting.

Suggested Reading

Fanatical Prospecting *by Jeb Blount*

Combo Prospecting *by Tony Hughes*

High-Profit Prospecting *by Mark Hunter and Mike Weinberg*

Predictable Prospecting *by Marylou Tyler and Jeremy Donovan*

CHAPTER 4

The Obvious Choice is not Always Obvious

Mountain Myles is my friend and drinking buddy. You may know him as the chatbot ninja, but more about that later. Mountain Myles is the modern-day Grizzly Adams of automated B2B marketing. Riding an electric bicycle to breeze past clogged traffic, Mountain Myles escaped the chaos of modern life with his dog and a 13-inch MacBook pro.

In the 1982 NBC TV series, an evil rancher accuses Grizzly Adams of murder, forcing him to escape into the Californian mountains to befriend a baby grizzly bear cub. The rancher captures Adams' daughter as bait to lure Adams into a deadly trap. In an expected turn of events, Adams exposes the evil rancher and proves his innocence. The story is about the fight between good and evil in the simplest form, but it contains other layers.

Understanding our deep innate connection to nature and leveraging this connection for survival empowers the legend of Grizzly Adams. In the same way, Mountain Myles struggled to survive in his everyday business like most other full-service marketing agencies. Escaping to the mountains, Myles found a stray puppy that led him inadvertently to chatbots. The dog helped

Myles reboot his life and survive on the new frontier. In honor of the TV series, Myles named his dog Grizzly.

Mountain Myles loves chatbots. For the people who don't know what a chatbot is: it is a software algorithm that simulates a conversation with a real person online. The business replaces people answering live chat questions with an intelligent software agent to save money. The chatbot is an example of the famous Turing test from artificial intelligence. The renowned mathematician and computer scientist Alan Turing proposed to define artificial intelligence as an operational performance test. If a real person participates in an online conversation and, after a specified period, cannot distinguish if the counterparty is a real person or software, then the Turing test is successful. The software has attained a realistic level of simulated human intelligence.

Mountain Myles promised a marvelous idea to save money and make money simultaneously. Imagine if a chatbot could converse with potential customers online, answer questions, and convert sales for only the cost of electricity; a marketer's dream come true! *Twenty-four-hour sales and support for virtually no cost.*

Swept up in the hype, I lost my senses and marched headlong into the valley of death with my buddy Mountain Myles. Facebook Messenger, driven by a happy little twenty-four-hour chatbot that never sleeps, seemed like a good idea at the time; it wasn't.

Myles created a Facebook that directed prospects to a Facebook Messenger chatbot. He meticulously planned the automatic conversation flow that was supposed to replace the human customer service agent. The Facebook ad worked well and delivered hundreds of leads, but the chatbot was a black hole for creating warm sales leads. It destroyed all life, and nothing escaped.

Myles' natural disposition befit a friendly Labrador. Usually, I would enjoy a coffee with Mountain Myles, but I was in a foul mood today. Nothing annoys me more than a marketing campaign with a zero result. It had been more than twenty years since I had scored a zero, and I hated the feeling of failure. I wanted to hear Mountain Myles' excuses, not to criticize him but to determine if the Facebook Messenger campaign was salvageable or if I should move to another social media platform.

"What would you like?" Mountain Myles asked me.

Resisting the cheap shot. I said, "A cappuccino, please."

"What type of milk?"

I replied, "No fat, please."

Barista Fiona played the coffee machine with a slow, noisy rhythm, allowing enough time for me to calm down.

After my first sip, I said, "Good coffee, Myles. You look like you have lost some weight; have you been hitting the gym?"

"No, just eating a bit less each meal."

Thanks, Myles. You left an excellent opening for me. I looked Myles in the face and said, "I think you have been eating my money with your Facebook ads. What do you think is happening?". After 15 minutes of complaining about Facebook, I gleaned that the recent changes made targeting businesses somewhat more difficult on the platform. That may be true, but I suspect that the real problem was not Facebook, but perhaps the Ninja was still wearing P-plates. I had heard enough to decide, and I said nothing critical, and we parted as friends.

The Fill-the-Pipe Program

Lecture 4: The LinkedIn Platform

"Before LinkedIn and other social networks, ABC stood for Always Be Closing in the sales world. Now, ABC means Always Be Connecting, because your connections lead to your next lead, and your next close."

Jill Rowley

Large social media platforms like Facebook, Instagram, and Twitter are intended to enable the public to connect and communicate, and they are not intended for business-to-business communication. HubSpot research found that LinkedIn is 277% more effective at generating leads than Facebook and Twitter. LinkedIn has emerged as the best-performing social media platform for B2B sales and marketing.

The LinkedIn Platform

- LinkedIn is a social media platform primarily used for professional networking, and the platform also provides functionality for sales, marketing, and career development.
- LinkedIn enables members to create profiles and send connection request invitations to other members. An accepted connection represents a virtual professional relationship.
- LinkedIn can also be used for:

- o Lead generation
- o Promote webinars and live events
- o Publish articles and posts
- o Join groups

The Rapid Growth of LinkedIn Membership

- LinkedIn was launched in May 2003, 9 months before Facebook. Membership has grown rapidly over the period, and in September 2021, LinkedIn surpassed 750 million registered members in over 200 countries, including 95 million senior-level roles and 65 million decision-makers globally.
- Australia is ranked 12th worldwide on LinkedIn membership with 12 million users.
- LinkedIn has more than 350 million active users, and on average, the user spends 17 minutes on LinkedIn each month.
- Only a tiny percentage of users share content regularly:
  - o Three million users share content weekly, and one million users have published an article.

About LinkedIn

- The LinkedIn headquarters are in Sunnyvale, California, and LinkedIn has more than 20,000 employees worldwide.
- Microsoft purchased LinkedIn for US$26.2 Billion in 2016.

- In 2021, LinkedIn's annual revenue exceeded US$10B per annum, and it generated US$160m in net income.
- LinkedIn's revenue is predominantly generated by selling member profile information to recruiters and sales and marketing professionals.

Member Information

- LinkedIn Profile Database
  - Members create a profile and enter their personal and company information
  - A tremendous amount of valuable and rich information is stored in the profiles
- The LinkedIn premium subscription (Sales Navigator) provides valuable information for marketers, and it is a critical tool for salespeople. Sales Navigator has become the de facto standard tool for B2B sales and marketing:
  - 76% of B2B content marketers use LinkedIn
  - 45% of marketers have acquired customers through the LinkedIn platform
  - 95% of B2B content marketers use LinkedIn for organic content marketing
  - 65% of B2B companies have used LinkedIn paid ads to acquire customers in the US
- LinkedIn is the top-rated social media platform for B2B.
- The B2B list provider industry (suppliers of marketing lists) has significantly declined as the Sales

Navigator subscription allows real-time dynamic prospect list generation.

LinkedIn is the Best Social Media Platform for B2B

- LinkedIn has emerged as the best performing social media platform for B2B sales and marketing, and currently, it has no noteworthy competitors.
- According to a HubSpot research, the LinkedIn platform has proven more effective at targeted lead generation than Facebook and Twitter.

Messaging Methods

- LinkedIn offers several methods to send messages to other members. The different types of messages include:
  o Connection Requests
  o Direct Messages
  o InMail
  o Posts
  o Paid Ads
- Your network on LinkedIn consists of:
  o 1st-degree connections
  o 2nd-degree connections
  o 3rd-degree connections
  o Followers
  o Fellow members of your LinkedIn groups
- You can build your network by:
  o Sending connection request (CR) invitations to connect with other members

- o Importing contact lists and automatically sending bulk CRs to the list
- o Accepting connections that have been sent to you
- o Joining groups
- o Attracting followers
- The degree (level) of connection affects how you are permitted to communicate with other members on LinkedIn.
- Direct Messages (DM) on LinkedIn are private messages sent from one member to another. It allows a member to communicate privately to another member, at no cost, if the other member is an existing connection.
- InMail in LinkedIn is a message that can be used to contact a member that is not a connection directly, and this is a cold reach-out message.
- Regular members are not permitted to send InMails. InMails are a premium feature that is part of the LinkedIn premium subscription. There is a low limit to the number of InMails that are allowed to be sent each month, thereby restricting the effectiveness of traditional cold marketing methods.

Track the Effectiveness of InMail Messages

- By using InMail, users get access to the InMail analytics page. This page provides detailed information about the messages users have sent, which can then be used for improving the messaging outreach and strategy.

- LinkedIn has established a professional code of conduct for communication between members. There are some basic rules for participating professionally on LinkedIn. Unlike Facebook and Twitter, where almost anything goes, the LinkedIn network is a professional network that engages in polite communication.
- Professional communication and polite language is critical in building effective lead generation campaigns on the LinkedIn platform. Chapter 9 discusses professional communication in detail.
- Code of conduct
  - https://legal.LinkedIn.com/content/dam/legal/LinkedIn_Partner_Code.pdf
- User agreement
  - https://www.LinkedIn.com/legal/user-agreement
- Service agreement
  - https://www.LinkedIn.com/legal/l/service-terms
- Common LinkedIn Agreements and Terms Summary
  - https://www.LinkedIn.com/help/LinkedIn/answer/4448/commonly-viewed-agreements-guidelines-policies-terms-and-conditions?lang=en

My disastrous foray with Mountain Myles graphically taught me that the best social media platform for B2B marketing is the LinkedIn platform, and the reason is apparent. The information stored in LinkedIn profiles enables LinkedIn to target prospects much more accurately than other social media platforms. People tend to use the LinkedIn platform during business hours at work. Therefore, members of the platform are much more open to engaging in work-related conversations than members of other social media platforms like Facebook or Instagram.

Experts are rarely good at implementing their expertise for themselves, like a painter's home in desperate need of a coat of paint. It isn't easy to be objective when emotionally attached and embroiled in the situation, and I suppose that is why doctors don't treat their own families.

For B2B sales and marketing professionals, social media and, in particular, LinkedIn will become a necessary tool within the next few years. The inevitable evolution brings the two-sided golden coin. Where tails is the threat, and heads is the opportunity. The threat and opportunity are distinguished by knowledge (in this case, power comes much later). By now, the *why* you need to change should be clear, understanding *what* and *how* transforms the threat into an opportunity and marks a bold step forward in the journey.

CHAPTER 5

Strategy

People become management consultants and business coaches for many different reasons. While some like the low-pressure lifestyle, others like the variety of work engagements. I love strategy and tactics. There is nothing more exciting than analyzing a business, establishing a personal connection with a sales director, and formulating an immediate plan to double sales revenue. The fundamentals and principles are standard, but the strategy is always very different. Even in the same industry, each business and leader are very different; the same approach rarely works well twice.

The Jaguar is a large feline predator native to the Americas. Six feet in length and 200 pounds of raw power, the Jaguar is the largest cat species in the Americas and is a celebrated hunter. The Jaguar's signature natural gift is that it has the strongest jaw of all cats. Preferring power to strategy, the animal crushes the skull of its prey in one enormously powerful stroke. Interestingly, the less powerful feline predators prefer to attack the softer area of the throat, achieving the same kill rate with a more subtle strategy. The Jaguar does not need a strategy with a surplus of power, or does he?

Jayden Shipper drove his new vehicle, a black Jaguar, into the closest car parking space to the office entrance. The Jaguar car salesman neglected to mention that reliability was not mandatory in the new car. It did, however, look great, and perhaps that was more important. After all, Jayden could afford two if need be. Sleek and powerful, the car reflected the newfound business success enjoyed by Jayden, having tolerated an ordinary Ford for the previous decade.

Mystery surrounded the miraculous growth of the software business. How could the Shipper Software business stagnate for more than a decade and suddenly grow like mushrooms after rain? The answer was stunningly simple. In fact, so simple that it wasn't believable.

Virtually all our clients follow the same pattern when we start working together. They only spend time thinking strategically about their business every fortnight when we meet for our 90-minute coaching sessions. Often it takes a few years to break this nasty habit, and for the clients that can break free from the daily minutia, the results are often breathtaking.

The Fill-the-Pipe Program

Lecture 5: What Is Strategy?

"Nothing is more critical for business success than creating a good strategy."

Chris Harasty

A professionally managed business requires several different forms of strategies. The business strategy determines the overall direction of the business. For example, is the business going to compete on 1. price, 2. differentiation, or

3. focused niche strategy. Another type of strategy is the marketing strategy. The marketing strategy enables a business to stand out and develop a competitive advantage. In this lecture, we will discuss the purpose of strategy and how to measure its impact.

What is Strategy, and Why is it Useful?

- People often confuse the two terms: strategy and tactics. Rather than provide a formal definition, we will explain the meaning of strategy with a powerful example.
- Hannibal was a Carthaginian general who lived from 247 – to 182 BC and became known for his brilliant and creative military strategy.

- Hannibal fought the Romans in the famous Battle of Cannae in 216 B.C. Outnumbered by almost 2 to 1, he developed a new revolutionary battle formation. The victory is still regarded as one of the best military victories of all time.
- Conventional military tactics required that the soldiers would line up next to each other in a straight line with multiple groups of soldiers aligned behind each other. The soldiers would march forward in a straight-line formation and fight the enemy who had the same formation. As the first line of soldiers fell, the line behind continued the fight on both sides. Therefore, the side with the largest army would always win the battle.

Traditional Battle Formation

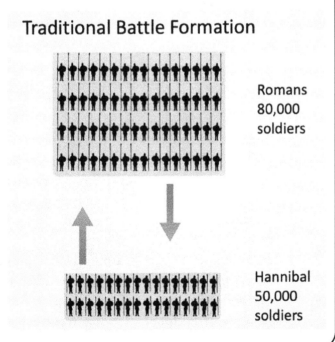

Romans 80,000 soldiers

Hannibal 50,000 soldiers

- Note that the structure of the traditional battle formations were static straight lines of soldiers engaging in battle.

New Strategy Battle Formation

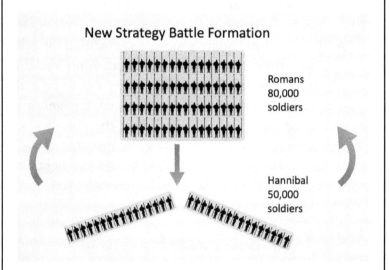

Romans
80,000
soldiers

Hannibal
50,000
soldiers

- Hannibal faced inevitable defeat with half the resources if he used the same traditional formation. Instead, he created a new battle formation that had never been used before.
- Roman military training dictated that soldiers pursue the retreating enemy. Thus, when Hannibal's first line of soldiers appeared to retreat, the Romans marched forward, leaving their side flanks exposed to Hannibal's army.
- In contrast, Hannibal's army did not pursue the retreating Romans. Instead, they attacked the rear of the Roman army. The Romans, confused by being attacked from both sides, were trounced.

Lucas Shipper, Jayden's father, started his software business in his home study. The early years were kind to Lucas, and the company grew steadily. In less than a decade, the business had grown to over $1m in revenue with ten busy staff members. As the years passed, Jayden more than earned his share and transitioned into the role of CEO. However, after an initial spurt, the business plateaued with 15 staff members and approximately $1.5m revenue per annum. Generating an average of $100,000 in revenue per employee, the company was barely breaking even, and it stagnated at this level for more than five years.

Jayden hired a support engineer to handle the constant flow of infuriating PC issues. Having ample free time, Jayden stopped firefighting and embraced the coach's advice to engage in quarterly strategic planning. To no one's surprise, the results were outstanding. The business grew in less than four years; Jayden made $6m in revenue annually and $3m+ in profit. The result was even more impressive because the revenue was high quality as the customers were mainly large corporations that signed long-term subscriptions. The annual revenue was predominantly recurrent, requiring no sales and marketing effort. We will learn how to generate high-quality revenue later in the book.

With such impressive success, was it time for Jayden to rest and enjoy life? While some of you may say *yes*, Jayden thought differently. He knew he had only just started and wondered how far he could go with his current strategy and game plan. What was the limit of his potential? What was the endpoint if he had achieved this much with only one simple strategy?

Jayden was fishing for accolades, and rightfully so.

"What do you think of the results?"

"Good."

"Have we now finished?"

"No, we have only just started."

"Really. So what is next?"

"That is what we will discuss in the next session."

CHAPTER 6

The Sales Revenue Maximizer Model

Oliver Steel towered above his staff of four hundred people; he was a tall, handsome man with imposing stature. His lush, brown hair was starting to thin, but this was the only visible sign of aging. At forty, most people begin to feel that the body has reached its peak, and the remaining years will reveal a multitude of aches and pain. Oliver didn't fit that mold; he was anything but ordinary.

Oliver had to learn to command attention early in life, being the middle sibling out of five energetic brothers. Otherwise, he would have gotten lost amidst the chaos. The business leader learned his craft; fighting his four brothers over toys developed a perfect crucible teaching him all about alliances, competitive strategies, and indispensable negotiating skills. And those of you with brothers know that brothers fight dirty, and even a slither of sentimentality is regarded as weakness personified. Life has a funny way of teaching you important lessons, doesn't it?

Oliver loved competition. He was fueled by a burning desire to win everything. It was a double-edged sword that drove the man; the feeling of winning was an unimaginable high and more addictive than drugs. Meanwhile, the negative emotions of losing felt unbearable. The high-octane fuel propelled Oliver with an unmatched motivation. In essence, losing motivated him to work hard, and winning made him seek a larger goal next time.

Oliver's fierce competitive drive was a natural fit for the business world. The more money he made, the more he could donate to the Church to do more good deeds. With that realization, Oliver's motivation was now turbo-charged, and it was also this spark that fueled his obsession with driving efficiency.

The benefit of business efficiency is obvious; if you can find a more efficient method to perform a process, you can reduce costs and make more money. So far, nothing new, right? However, Oliver taught me what obsession with efficiency could produce. It was nothing short of a miracle.

Assume that you have a staff of a hundred working in an admin team. The business has invested money in developing custom software that helps the team do their work. Oliver would discuss every detail of this software. He spent hours fussing over screen designs down to the last pixel. You know what they say; the devil lies in the details. Joy was when Oliver eliminated the need to move to a new screen and combine data fields onto a single screen. Excitement abounded when an additional three or four mouse clicks were eliminated in a process because that may save five or ten seconds in a 60-second task.

I thought the fixation on efficacy might be pathological until Oliver showed me the calculation:

Item	Result
100 staff members, including benefits + oncosts @ $100K each per annum	$10m per annum in wages
That small optimization process done 100-200 times a day saves about 1 hour per day	
1 hour x 200 days x 100 staff	20,000 hours
20,000 hours @ $55 per hour	$1.1m costs saved each year

Which, for Oliver, meant that he could indulge in skiing in Aspen with his young family.

When Chris, the master coach, allows himself, he can learn from the client. Based on this powerful optimization lesson, I took the next step and created the concept of the Profit Chain, the topic of the following lecture.

The Fill-the-Pipe Program

Lecture 6: The Sales Revenue Maximizer

"If you can't measure it, you can't improve it."

Peter Drucker

Financial models measure and monitor daily, monthly, and quarterly performance. The indicators are often called *Key Performance Indicators* or *KPIs*. KPIs are used extensively in business to monitor the health of a business and determine bottlenecks and areas of potential growth.

What are Key Performance Indicators?

- Key Performance Indicators (KPI) are metrics that a business uses to identify if it is on track to achieve its goals and objectives. For example, the business may want to know how much sales revenue has been created from last month's marketing spend.
- A common KPI is *Return on Investment* (ROI). Sales managers will often track the ROI of various projects, and the data becomes one of the factors that inform business and investment decisions. For example, marketing managers will often focus on improving the customers' experiences, believing that a good customer experience may encourage repeat business. In this case, the NPS *Net Promoter Score* is a common KPI or metric used to measure customer experience. Sales Managers are often interested in the cost per lead (CPL) KPI.

- A business will generate large volumes of data. KPIs are intended as a shortcut or summary of the most critical elements of the business. KPIs provide a convenient way to analyze and track the performance of the business while it is in motion; they highlight areas of the business that can improve.
- Choosing which KPIs to track will depend on the business objectives and the strategies and tactics implemented.

Characteristics of KPIs

- Tracking KPIs is similar to tracking personal goals. Therefore, the SMART principles can make the KPIs more effective.
- The SMART acronym means:
  - Specific: What is it measuring?
  - Measurable: Can it be tracked?
  - Achievable: Is this measurement attainable?
  - Realistic: Are we looking at a practical KPI?
  - Timely: Can we look at this in a reasonable period?

Why are KPIs Important?

- KPIs in business are important for several reasons:
  - Required for performance management.
  - KPIs help teams know what they are doing well and what needs work.
  - Help achieve business objectives.

    KPIs help keep staff focused on the same goal, increasing overall efficiency.

o Improve staff morale.
o Since KPIs are measurable, positive outcomes can be celebrated and rewarded, giving employees a greater sense of responsibility,

• Usually, a business analyst (who could also be the CFO) will build the financial growth model for the organization to follow.

The Profit Chain Model

• A simple model of the business is called the Profit Chain Model. If you imagine that a business is a machine, then the profit creation process follows the nine stages of the Profit Chain Model shown in figure 1 below.

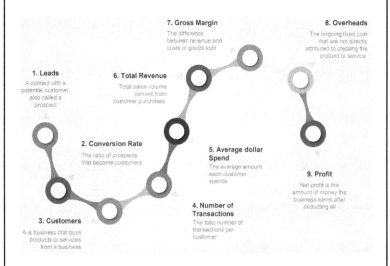

Figure 1. The Profit Chain Model

- The Profit Chain Model is a simplified model of a running business. Although large companies have more complex relationships that influence the organization, the profit chain model is still valid.

Increasing Sales Revenue

- Based on the Profit Chain model, you can create simple KPIs to monitor the performance of the business. For our purpose, we will focus on KPIs that help us with increasing sales revenue.
- Often existing customers have a fixed spending pattern, and it is quite challenging to increase the spending on your current customers. For example, if your business supplies raw materials to manufacturers, the manufacturers will only purchase more if their demand increases.
- Often the best way to grow revenue is for the business to get new customers, and that is why businesses tend to put some or much effort and focus on new customer acquisition.
- Recall the new customer acquisition paradox discussed previously. New customer acquisition tends to be the most prominent factor that can increase sales revenue, but it also tends to be the most difficult to achieve; the paradox is that the best growth method is the most difficult to achieve.
- The new customer acquisition paradox raises the key question: *What is the most efficient way to achieve a new customer acquisition level?*

The Key to New Customer Acquisition

- In many businesses, the principal factor that increases sales revenue is new customer acquisition, and the most critical factor that enables new customer acquisition is lead generation. Therefore, an oversupply of new warm leads is the critical success factor required to generate sales growth with new customer acquisition.
- To understand this relationship, we can investigate a small subset of the Profit Chain financial model that focuses on the critical elements of new customer acquisition. The financial model is called the Sales Rep Maximizer.

The Sales Revenue Maximizer Model

- The Sales **Revenue** Maximizer model is shown in an excel spreadsheet in Figure 1. The input fields are highlighted in grey.
- The fill-the-pipe program uses LinkedIn to generate warm leads. The cost of this program and other similar programs is $24,000 per annum plus $1,000 per annum for the LinkedIn premium subscription.

Figure 1. The Sales Revenue Maximizer Financial Model

The Sales Revenue Maximizer Financial Model		
Costs		
Sales Rep Wages		$0
On costs	0%	$0
Total Cost		$0
Average Prospecting Time	0%	$0
Cost of fill-the-pipe		$24,000
Cost Saving		-$24,000
Sales		
Sales Budget		$1,000,000
Average Sales Rep	0%	$0
Extra Selling Time	0%	
Extra Sales	0%	$0
Total Sales		$0
Cost		$24,000
Return on Investment		
ROI		0.0

- The input values will vary for each business, but many of the values are similar. The typical values are shown below in Table 1.

Table 1. Typical values

Data Field	Typical Value
Salesperson Wages	$100,000 per annum
On-costs	30%
Average Time Spent Prospecting	40%
The Cost of the Fill-the-Pipe Program	$24,000
Sales Budget	$1,000,000 Per annum
Average Sales Rep Achievement	80%
Extra Selling Time	30%

- The website www.payscale.com shows that the salary range for a Business Development Manager in the US is from $75,000 to $150,000 per annum, and we select $100,000 per annum to make the calculations simple.
- Oncosts vary from 25% to 45%; we select 30% as a conservative figure.
- The average salesperson spends about 40% of their time prospecting during regular business hours.
- An outsourced lead generation program, on average, costs about $24,000 per annum and should free up about 30% of the salesperson's time that was previously spent on prospecting tasks.

- Based on 30% extra time, the model assumes that the salesperson can sell an equal amount more deals as they have an oversupply of warm leads. The result of the model is shown below in Figure 3.

Figure 3. Typical results

The Sales Revenue Maximizer Financial Model		
Costs		
Sales Rep Wages		$100,000
On costs	30%	$30,000
Total Cost		$130,000
Average Prospecting Time	40%	$52,000
Cost of fill-the-pipe		$24,000
Cost Saving		$28,000
Sales		
Sales Budget		$1,000,000
Average Sales Rep	80%	$800,000
Extra Selling Time	30%	
Extra Sales	30%	$300,000
Total Sales	110%	$1,100,000
Cost		$24,000
Return on Investment		
ROI		12.5

The Results

- The lead generation program costs $24,000 per annum, enabling the salesperson to spend 30% more time selling and closing deals, instead of prospecting.
- The result is an additional $300,000 per annum in sales revenue.
- The return on investment (ROI) is > 10%.

Summary of Key Points

- KPIs are convenient metrics that summarize the health of the business.
- The Sales Maximizer model shows that an oversupply of leads will significantly increase sales.

CHAPTER 7

1-a-Week

Amelia Haddin's passion for fast cars stemmed from her father, Todd Haddin. Todd always wanted to be a champion race car driver, but unfortunately, he did not have the talent or dedication to prevail. Amelia was conceived on a wild night filled with alcohol and passion after a hard-fought victory in the local derby. Todd responded to the newfound responsibility nobly by marrying the mother and giving up his Formula One dream for a sensible job. Weekends consisted of endless motorsports on cable TV. Longing for attention, Amelia learned quickly that Todd was always happy to talk about motorsports but lacked even the most rudimentary knowledge of Disney Princesses.

At work, Amelia was suffering the plight of the archetypal business development manager. Six weeks before the end of the quarter, her pipeline was strong, or so everyone said. Her close friend Jennifer said it was solid, and even her sales manager, Alan, said it looked ok. Over $1m of qualified opportunities, and her sales quota was only $375,000 – it should have been a walk in the park.

It was a Friday, and it felt like the worst day of her life. The proud pipeline melted on the hot summer day. *Gone, just vanished.* Friday was the worst day for the bad news. It presented two days of rest wasted obsessing about something she couldn't do anything about. The irony was that it wasn't her fault; everything happened so fast that it seemed to be an event beyond human comprehension. A series of events in her work had moved things beyond her control. How could she have predicted that George Demos would be stood down on allegations of sexual misconduct and Alan Andrews would be transferred to run the factory in Italy? What were the odds that Lisa Gardner would not get board approval for the most minor project she had ever presented? Lisa was the chosen one; she always got everything she asked for.

A distressed Amelia arrived ten minutes late to our Monday morning sales coaching session. Her mind was focused on her impending demise, and she was in a foul mood. However, a Master Coach does not react in such a situation. His first task is to provide empathy and make sure the individual feels like they are heard. Amelia needed to vent her intense emotions, but we couldn't stay in the problem space for too long. That is the mistake counselors often make. Staying in the mirky problem space for too long often worsens the problem. It is quite an art to pick the right time, and, most certainly, it was well before Amelia wanted to stop venting her frustration when I switched to solution-focused mode.

Have you ever wondered why it is so difficult to find a solution to your dire problems when you are under excessive stress? And just then comes an independent third person, suggesting reasonable options in minutes. Professor Barbara Fredrickson, a renowned social psychologist from the University of North Carolina, published the famous broaden-and-build theory in 2001.

Social psychology proposes that emotions prepare the body psychologically and physically to act in predefined ways. For example, anger creates the urge to attack, while fear causes an urge to escape.

Although this explanation sounds reasonable, what happens with positive emotions? Emotions like joy and gratitude don't seem as helpful as fear and anger. If positive emotions are not linked to survival, what is their purpose? Fredrickson developed the broaden-and-build theory to explain how positive emotions were important to survival.

The theory suggests that positive emotions expand awareness and encourage novel, exploratory thoughts, and actions. This expanded behavior builds valuable skills and psychological resources that, over time, enhance survival. In contrast, negative emotions have a more immediate effect, and they tend to narrow thinking, restrict options, and invoke survival instincts that drive rash behaviors. For example, anxiety leads to a specific fight-or-flight response.

Moving back to Amelia, all I had to do was temporarily calm her intense emotions and move into solution-focused mode and start to develop some options with her support. I always begin the process with a few ideas and then let the client take over once they realize that some options could work. By the end of the coaching session, we had a viable plan which had a reasonable chance of success. If I was to quantify the odds, there was a 40% chance that it could work, and Amelia would survive to fight another day.

So, what was the plan? It was simple, merely the beginning elements of the fill-the-pipe program. Fortunately, Amelia discovered the solution by herself. Self-discovery tends to motivate people more than being told the answer by a coach. Discussing a solution tends to be a delicate process where many psychological factors are balanced to achieve the desired outcome. Amelia needed to walk away from the coaching session with a viable plan that would work and a sense of hope and excitement that she may be able to achieve her goal if she moved into action. In this case, that would be survival.

Amelia's Tesla was back on the racetrack. Although Tesla had not yet released the self-driving functionality, driving the car was still pure excitement. The raw power of the acceleration was thrilling, and the feeling was almost as good as closing a big sale. For the rest of the afternoon, racing was a welcome diversion from the stress of work.

Amelia knew deep in her heart that the fill-the-pipe program was the long-term answer to the constant grind of achieving her quarterly sales budget. Meanwhile, what could she do to save herself now?

The Fill-the-Pipe Program

Lecture 7: The 1-a-Week Prospecting Approach

"Concentrate all your thoughts on the work at hand. The sun's rays do not burn until brought to a focus."

Alexander Graham Bell

The 1-a-week prospecting approach is the second step to building the system. It uses a simple and effective prospecting strategy that enables salespeople to double their sales in 12-24 months. Expressed simply, after 30 weeks of implementing the 1-a-week approach, the salesperson should have developed a sales pipeline that is four to six times the size of the typical sales pipeline. Over the next 12 months, the salesperson will be able to multiply their sales quota without discounting or implementing any special closing techniques.

The Pareto Principle

- The **Pareto principle** was developed by Joseph Juran (1904–2008), the Romanian-born American management consultant. Juran applied the work of the Italian economist Vilfredo Pareto to business practices. In 1896, Pareto found that approximately 80% of the land in Italy was owned by 20% of the people. He then generalized the concept and proposed that this ratio applies to many different business areas.
- The Pareto Principle, also known as the 80/20 rule, states that roughly 80% of outcomes are derived from 20% of the inputs. For example, 80% of sales come from 20% of customers.

Customer Segmentation

- Customer segmentation refers to separating customers into groups for analysis and business improvement. The segmentation is often based on revenue spent and symbolized with a letter of the alphabet.
  - A – The top customer segment that spends the most with the business
  - B – The 2nd best customer segment
  - C – The 3rd best customer segment
  - D – The bottom customer segment that spends the least
- Businesses tend to use the classifications to determine which segment to target in marketing campaigns.

Common Business Chaos

- Businesses accept all orders for any customer segment. The customers will be geographically and demographically diverse. This approach may maximize revenue, but it may not profit because different customer segments will have different delivery cost structures. The wide range of orders from different customer segments creates a challenge in developing an efficient delivery system.
- A more effective method is to plan which customer segment generates the most profit and focus on this segment. Subsequently, this helps businesses expand to other customer segments after optimizing the delivery system.
- The business needs to plan the business model in detail and understand the following information:
  - Which customer segment adds the most value to the business?
  - What is the ideal customer profile?
  - How does the business compare with the competition?
  - How does the business differentiate?
- A simple optimization scheme is described below using the Pareto principle.
- Using the Pareto principle, it is often the case that:
  - The A customer segment provides 80% of the business's total revenue
  - The D customer segment accounts for only 20% of the revenue but accounts for 80% of the problems in the business

- Over-discounting is where the price charged by the business is overly influenced by the D customer segment, neglecting the fact that the other customer segments could pay more for the same product or service.
- The D customer segment is often very price-sensitive and vocal. The common mistake businesses make is that they listen to the D customers and base pricing for all customer segments on the opinion of the vocal, price-sensitive D customers. This strategy will significantly reduce the total revenue earned by the business as A and B customers pay considerably more than D customers.
  - o D consumes more resources per transaction than the other customer segments and, therefore, is less profitable.
- Discounting practices need to be applied with caution. For example,
  - o assuming a business has $250,000 revenue and a 50% gross margin, a 10% discount means that the business needs to sell $62,500 more to achieve the same amount of gross profit
- Often, when the business increases prices by 10%, the bottom D customers drop off, but the same amount of sales revenue and profit is generated. However, a fortunate side effect is that the business loses the customer segment that causes the most issues.

- With a 10% higher margin, the business has more resources to provide better quality customer delivery. Therefore, customer satisfaction will increase when the business earns a higher margin (sells at a higher price).

Identify the Ideal Prospect

- Prospecting is time-consuming, and identifying the ideal customer profile is necessary to guide the process to save time efficiently. The ideal prospect is the same as the ideal customer, and it is where the business can deliver the most customer value and solve a critical customer need.
- Independent market research is often used to determine the:
  o Specific target market
  o How the product meets customer requirements
  o Perceived benefits of the product
  o How much the customer is prepared to pay
  o The viability of launching new products
- Other helpful information includes:
  o Strategic goals of the prospect
  o Business priorities
  o Budgets
  o Industry trends
  o Market trends
  o Competitive environment
- Once you have identified the ideal customer, you will be able to focus time on prospects who are more likely to become your customers.

The Tier-1 Target

- Assuming a salesperson's annual quota is $1m per annum. A tier-1 prospect is a business with the following criteria:
  - Has the requirement to spend over $200K per annum on your products and services
  - The prospect spends approximately $20K per month every month.
  - The $200K purchase is not one large transaction, but rather the spend is split relatively evenly over 12 months.

Tier-1 Prospecting Approach

- The Tier-1 prospecting approach is composed of five components:
  1. Big Target
  2. High-Quality Communication
  3. Low Volume Activity
  4. Demonstrating Expertise
  5. Conversion Patience

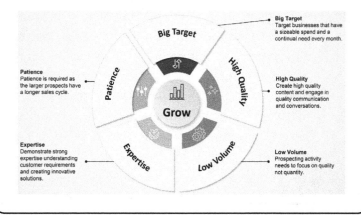

- **The Big Target** – The salesperson needs to focus on the appropriate target. Target businesses need to spend over $200K per annum ($20K per month).
- **High-quality communication** – High-quality communication and conversations with the prospect are essential for a salesperson.
- **Low Volume Activity** – Activity needs to focus on quality, not quantity.
- **Demonstrating Expertise** – Demonstrate expertise in solving customer problems with innovative solutions.
- **Conversion Patience** - Patience is required as the larger targets have a longer sales cycle.

The 1-a-Week approach

- The objective of the 1-a-week approach is to book one face-to-face appointment with a tier-1 prospect every week.
- After 30 weeks, the salesperson has met with thirty tier-1 prospects.
- Assuming that the salesperson is adequately trained in the product and can execute a good sales process (see the *Explode Your Sales* course), the average close rate is approximately 1/3. Therefore, about ten prospects will purchase and become customers.
- These ten customers will spend approximately $200K per annum with the business, and over the next 12 months, the salesperson will sell over $2m worth of new business.

> **Summary of Key Points**
>
> - The Pareto Principle states that roughly 80% of outcomes are derived from only 20% of the inputs.
> - Using the Pareto principle, it is often the case that:
>   - The A customer segment generates 80% of the business's total revenue
>   - The D customer segment accounts for only 20% of the revenue but accounts for 80% of the problems in the business
> - The objective of the 1-a-week approach is to book one face-to-face appointment with a tier-1 prospect every week.
> - After approximately thirty weeks, about ten customers will start purchasing, and over the next 12 months, revenue will double as long as delivery exceeds customer expectations.

A week before the end of the quarter, the drought broke. The dry land in the Midwest was drowning in the severe lack of water. After five years of virtually no rain, young children emerged from their homes at the sight of water pouring down – something they had never experienced. Water sustains life, and this time, it was no different. The rain would last for many weeks, and the drought would be lifted.

The fill-the-pipe program motivated Amelia to continue striving when everything seemed hopeless. It gave Amelia a clear vision of what she could achieve and the steps on how to get there. When fortune smiled and the drought broke, Amelia was ready to make the most of the opportunity.

Business confidence surged in the farming communities of the Northwest Territories and parts of the Great Plains. Amelia was able to salvage a few deals and post 81% of her quota with the grace of an extra week allowed by Alan. The extra week was enough to get over the 80% barrier, which was the threshold for an automatic performance review.

Amelia thanked God and vowed never to go through the same pain again. A deep burning motivation inside Amelia embraced the fill-the-pipe program. Rather than thinking about survival, Amelia now wants to become an elite salesperson that can rise above these challenges.

CHAPTER 8

Profile Optimization

"Where do I start?" Asked Emma, the new sales director.

"At the beginning," I said.

"Where is the beginning?"

"At the start."

"Are you being difficult on purpose?" Emma asked.

"Yes," I replied.

"Why?"

"To make a point that you won't forget."

"Ok, you have done that. Now please answer the question!"

"The answer is anywhere."

"Do you want me to cancel your next payment?"

Ignoring the jibe, I answered, "Good, now I have your attention. The answer is anywhere, and you must understand this point. I will give you an example of what I mean. Imagine you have a round birthday cake, and you are about to slice it. Where do you start? The answer is anywhere – if you keep going. If you don't keep going, then the answer is nowhere."

Emma looked puzzled, so I continued.

"As long as you keep going and keep doing things, it doesn't matter where you start. It just matters that you keep going."

With the frustration slowly abating, Emma tried again. "Ok, I will ask a different question. What is the best place to start?"

I said, "At the start… Only joking. The best place to start is by creating your best self."

Ambiguity overwhelmed Emma; were we still playing games, or was this a profound answer?

The Fill-the-Pipe Program

Lecture 8: Profile Optimization

"Your LinkedIn profile represents your personal brand, and it needs to show something special, and it is the cornerstone of effective LinkedIn lead generation campaigns."

Chris Harasty

A LinkedIn profile is the centerpiece of LinkedIn communication strategies. When a user sends a connection request, posts something, or runs a paid ad, the recipient will review the sender's profile before they respond. Therefore, the quality of the LinkedIn profile is an essential factor in the success of any lead generation campaign.

The Purpose of Profile Optimization

- Positive member interactions rely on a well-optimized LinkedIn profile. The profile showcases your personal brand, and it builds trust with the viewing member.
- A strong personal brand and a well-optimized profile are the foundation of an effective LinkedIn lead generation process. Without a good profile, lead generation campaigns will struggle.
- Profile optimization requires four main components:
  - Planning
  - Content structure
  - Keywords
  - Tools
- The information in the profile needs to be:
  - Completed
  - Correct
  - Relevant
  - Accurate (no exaggeration or false information)

Optimization Steps

- **Completing your profile**
  - The profile needs to be fully completed, and it should highlight your personal brand, accomplishments, experience, and recommendations.

- **Choose relevant keywords**
  - LinkedIn uses keywords to match relevant information across millions of professionals and job roles.

- Keywords can be thought of as unique tokens that represent a distinct concept. For LinkedIn, the concept is usually a specific business skill that can be used as a reference point to compare member profiles.
- Keywords should be inserted at the profile's beginning, middle, and end. The LinkedIn search algorithm will place a higher priority on this type of profile.
- Do not use exact keywords more than three or four times for every 500 words. Keyword stuffing (overuse) should be avoided.

- **How do you find keywords?**
  - Make a list of the services that you offer.
  - Software tools like SEMrush, Supple, and many others can provide a list of common keyword searches.

- **Elements of a LinkedIn profile**
  - *The Profile Picture*
    - A professional business photo from a professional photographer is strongly recommended. A clear headshot with a smile works the best.
    - A high-quality picture with a simple background is the minimum required.
  - *Header text or headline*
    - The headline is the most vital part to be optimized. Keywords can be placed in the headline. The message needs to be presented professionally. Professional communication is discussed in the following lecture.

- *Introduction*
  - LinkedIn prefers users to add basic information in this section.
- *Cover Image*
  - LinkedIn banners or cover images draw attention and showcase credibility. Professional cover images attract prospects and inspire members to contact you.
  - Consider adding the following to the cover image:
    - ➢ Business name
    - ➢ Website link
    - ➢ Social media handles
    - ➢ Your tagline or a brief call out to your target audience and how you can help them
    - ➢ For an example of a banner, see: https://www.linkedin.com/in/chrisharasty/

- **The *About* Section**
  - The about section is the most prominent profile section, and it occupies the largest space; this section is where achievements are highlighted. The *About* section should be written professionally and grab the audience's attention.
  - Some items that should be added include:
    - ➢ A benefit statement for the products and services represented.
    - ➢ WIIFM (What's In It For Me) for the target audience.
    - ➢ The value delivered to the target market.

➢ Note: it must not be written in a *salesy* language.

- **Featured**

  This section demonstrates the best work or results that have been delivered. LinkedIn provides options to add any of the following in the featured section:

  o Posts
  o Articles
  o Any media, such as photos, documents, or presentations
  o Testimonials from successful clients

- **Background**

  o **Work experience** – The experience section shows expertise and credibility in the field.
  o **Education** – Education details add value to the profile and assist LinkedIn searches.
  o **Licenses & certifications** – Special licenses or certificates should be added in this section.

- **Skills**

  o The skills listed help other members understand your capabilities and enhance the profile's credibility.

- **Recommendations**

  o The *Recommendations* section is an integral part of the profile, and it provides other members the opportunity to provide testimonials and enhances credibility.
  o Recommendations need to be strategically acquired and managed.

○ Recommendations need to be relevant to the target audience.

Summary of Key Points

- The LinkedIn profile is the centerpiece of LinkedIn communication strategies. When a user sends a connection request, posts, or runs a paid ad, the recipient will review the sender's profile before they respond.
- The quality of the LinkedIn profile is an essential factor in the success of any lead generation campaign.

Coaching practice needs to be informed by evidence-based coaching psychology. The theories are elaborate, interrelated, and work very effectively. But it is not all about clinical evidence-based processes, and pure clinical practice rarely delivers growth. Clients are human, and the Master Coach understands people.

The missing magical ingredient is the artistic side of coaching: theatre. I love the theatre. A fascination with elegant tactics and strategy started my voyage, and the theatre was a beautiful, unexpected friend I discovered on the journey.

Theatre emboldens the young Master from good to great. Without the substance of evidence-based practice, the theatre is empty; together, you have perhaps a blockbuster.

"Hi Emma, how are you today?" I asked Emma.

"I am well. I have finished my profile. What do you think?" She replied.

"It is good, but now we need to road-test it."

"What do you mean?"

"What is important is not whether I like it, but if your ideal customer likes it."

"Ok, so where do I start?" Emma asked.

"At the beginning," I joked.

"Uhh!"

"Sorry, I couldn't resist. How many tier-1 customers do you have at the moment?"

"Maybe four or five."

"That is a good place to start, and five should be enough."

"Ok, I will send them an email and a link to review,"

"What else could you do that may be better?"

"Not sure."

"How about you give them a call and discuss with them over the phone?" I asked.

"But that will take a lot more time," Emma replied.

"Yes, and that is why I want you to do it."

"You want me to waste my time."

"Yes."

"Why would you want me to do that?"

"Because that is your homework and next week, we will discuss what happened. Is that ok with you?"

"Ok, but it sounds silly," Emma commented.

"Sometimes silly is good," I said

Coaching a client is like getting your teenager to clean their bedroom or do the dishes once a year. Usually, there is resistance every step of the way, even when they know that it is good for them; that is the cross that parents bear. Fortunately, children grow up to become parents, and the inevitable angst is passed forward. I wish my progeny only happiness and good fortune, but that doesn't exclude a measured dose of angst for my little darlings.

Vertical growth is the most difficult to achieve, while horizontal growth is much easier. Transformation is a vertical development activity, and resistance abounds. I love vertical coaching, not because of the challenge but rather the quantum results. Of course, the client experiences pain (not me), but the result is electric and always worthwhile. It marks a level the client would not be able to achieve by themselves, which makes me feel special. It is difficult to describe: exhilarating, satisfying, intense, and addictive. That can't be work; it must be fun, and it is.

Emma is on the verge of taking a small vertical jump; having sold small accounts during her career, she does not yet understand how to manage tier-1 accounts. I am optimistic that Emma will ring the epiphany bell next week, at least once. If not, I will lightly tap the bell for her.

CHAPTER 9

Professional Communication

Film critics agree that *When Harry Met Sally* reaches the summit (not climax) of romantic comedies. The film explores the question, *Can guys and girls ever truly be friends?* Nora Ephron's screenplay delivers in spades, and the superb performances by Meg Ryan and Billy Crystal combine to create a hilarious masterpiece.

The typical romantic comedy conforms to a standard plot. A young man and woman are portrayed as likable individuals suited for each other. The audience wants them to be together. Yet circumstances prevent the union. Can the young couple overcome the obstacles? Will there be a fairy-tale happy ending?

In the business world, sellers and buyers are different parties that form a union when a purchase is transacted, and sometimes a strong business relationship is formed. Elite salespeople understand that selling is about communication and connection with the seller, courting rituals without the benefits.

Alicia Foster is the sales director of an office equipment supplier. Office equipment is an industry with a twist. Every business needs a photocopier, but no one needs it now. This strange paradox means selling office equipment and reaching the sales budget are easy and difficult tasks simultaneously. It should be easy because every business needs the equipment, but it is also problematic because the prospect can postpone the decision indefinitely.

"Chris, how do I stop prospects from wasting our time? It is difficult to get an appointment, so my salespeople will talk to anyone who says yes, but most of the time, the prospect has no real interest in buying office equipment," Alicia said.

"Good question. Alicia, if you solved this problem, what percentage of time would your salespeople save?" I asked her.

"Depends on the salesperson. Maybe 25 to 50%."

"So, it is worth training and putting a system together to help?"

With a grimace, Alicia said, "Stop selling to me. Yes, of course, it is. But I will not do anything until I am sure the system will work."

"Of course, Alicia. Do you have any salespeople who naturally do it well and don't waste their time on useless appointments?" I inquired.

"Yes, Adrian is good at that. Not perfect, but good," Alicia said.

Finding a way forward, I said, "Ok, I will have a chat with Adrian."

"Chris, I can do that myself. What else can you tell me?"

Focusing on the issue, I asked, "What would you class as a waste of time?"

Forcefully stating the issues she wanted to be solved, Alicia said, "When a salesperson has a sales appointment, the prospect is not looking for a photocopier and does not have a budget."

"Ok, that is pretty clear. Do you have a salesperson who can go to an appointment like that and still make a sale?" I asked.

"Yes, we have one: Frank. Frank can do that."

With my curiosity peaked, I asked, "Does Frank ever miss his sales budget?"

"Never."

"Do I have permission to be a bit controversial?" I asked Alicia.

"Maybe..." She responded.

"I suspect Frank doesn't qualify his appointments. And I suspect Frank can sell to prospects that don't have a need and don't have a budget. Is that correct?"

"Yes, sometimes. Not always." Alicia responded.

"Do you know why?" I challenged.

"No, that is why I am talking to you," Alicia responded, frustrated.

"The reason is that Frank is good at building relationships quickly when he sits in front of the prospect is because he can create the need to purchase a product or service, and if the need is strong enough, the prospect will find the budget. They just take the money from somewhere else."

"Maybe..." Alicia wasn't convinced.

"So, perhaps the problem is that your salespeople are not making the most out of the sales appointments, but remember, we can still do the sales qualification you are looking for," I added.

Alicia was skeptical. "The two ideas are very different. How is that going to work?"

"That is easier than you think. All we need to do is teach your salespeople to *fall in love at first sight* with the prospect."

"How do you do that?" Alicia seemed inquisitive now.

"The first step is to get the sales appointment, which happens with professional communication...."

The Fill-the-Pipe Program

Lecture 9: Professional Communication

"A professional must be an expert in their specialist field and always act in their client's interests. Elevating the client's interest includes withdrawing from a sale if the product or service does not suit the customer's requirements."

Chris Harasty

Perhaps the most challenging thing to learn for LinkedIn users who are not from a traditional professional background (like a doctor or lawyer) is the style of communication required on LinkedIn. This platform expects a different communication style from other social media platforms like

Facebook or Twitter; members must avoid being salesy, pushy, generic, or annoying. Standard cold marketing communication is not considered acceptable on the LinkedIn platform, and LinkedIn will restrict the account if such behavior is reported or detected. In this lecture, we will describe the term *professional* and how to engage in professional communication that is compliant with LinkedIn's published code of conduct.

LinkedIn: Code of Conduct

- LinkedIn has established a strict professional code of conduct for communication between members. There are rules for participating professionally on LinkedIn, unlike on Facebook and Twitter, where communication is rarely moderated or censored. The LinkedIn network expects positive and respectful communication.
- LinkedIn code of conduct
  o https://legal.LinkedIn.com/content/dam/legal/ LinkedIn_Partner_Code.pdf
- LinkedIn User agreement
  o https://www.LinkedIn.com/legal/ user-agreement
- LinkedIn Service agreement
  o https://www.LinkedIn.com/legal/l/ service-terms
- Common LinkedIn Agreements and Terms Summary

- https://www.LinkedIn.com/help/LinkedIn/answer/4448/commonly-viewed-agreements-guidelines-policies-terms-and-conditions?lang=en

What is a Profession?

- The Council of Professionals defines a profession as a disciplined group of individuals who adhere to a common code of conduct and ethical standards. The professionals have learned expert knowledge and skills that are taught and recognized by a high level of education delivered by universities or other colleges of advanced education.
- The conduct of professionals is monitored by a professional body that requires high standards of behavior in the services delivered to clients and the relationships with other colleagues.
- A professional is required to act in the interest of their client, and a professional will not perform a service that is not in the best interests of their client. For example, a doctor will not operate on a patient and take out their appendix if it is not needed. This behavior may contrast with some salespeople who will try and maximize revenue by trying to upsell and cross-sell other products and services, even if it is not in the client's interest.
- Professions are regulated with strict rules of membership. They have significant barriers to entry and are marked by formal university training and enforced by legal sanctions for unethical conduct.

- Examples of professionals include doctors, lawyers, and accountants. Many other job roles act as semi-professionals; although they do not necessarily have a professional body that regulates their practice, they can still voluntarily act professionally. For example, salespeople do not have a professional governing body, but many salespeople voluntarily act ethically.

What is Professional Writing?

- Professional writing is a type of writing that utilizes a formal style commonly used in the business environment. It is predominantly used at work to communicate important information clearly and concisely.
- Professional writing is short and crisp because it is written to be read rapidly. Business executives are often very busy, and they want to be able to scan documents. For example, these lecture notes are presented in point form so that the reader can quickly grasp the information.
- Professional writing is different from creative writing. At times, creative writing uses ambiguous language, slowly reveals a plot, and develops characters throughout the book.

Professional Writing Style

- Academic writing is similar to professional writing. It has a formal tone, albeit difficult to understand for most people outside of its field of expertise. Professional writing is easily graspable.

- The formal tone avoids the use of slang terms. The grammar and spelling will be accurate, and the language will not use exaggeration or hype. The language avoids salesy or pushy messages.
- Professional writing also utilizes the first-person point of view. Personal pronouns will be used, including *me, I, mine, our, we, us,* and *ours.* It also uses terms that the reader will be able to understand easily.
- Being concise is key to effective professional communication. The writer needs to avoid:
  o Repetitive language
  o Artistic language
    ▪ metaphors, rhyme schemes, and other literary devices are not used
- Professional writing is objective, fair, unemotional, and factual – note that your biases are omitted. For example, you would not write the following message: "We have the best accounting service in the world" because of the biasedness of the situation.
- Formal writing is thorough and accurate. It is based on research, but it does not need to include references like academic writing.
- In LinkedIn messages, the content needs to be customized for different persons, and it cannot be generic and based on hype and exaggeration. Standard cold marketing communication is not acceptable on the LinkedIn platform with direct message communication.

Professional Writing Examples

- Below is an example of unprofessional writing that uses exaggeration, hype, and scarcity:

  Enjoy the best legal advice in the US.

  Special Offer - First 10 hours come with a 50% discount.

  Hurry up! Only the first ten qualify for the special offer.

- An example of professional writing is:

  Hi XXXX,

  Traditionally IAST tools have been plagued with the challenges of scalability and accuracy.

  The article below describes how to solve these challenges.

  www.yourwebsite/article01

  If you'd like more information, we can have a brief chat next week.

  What day/time suits you next week?

  Regards,
  Chris

LinkedIn Etiquette

- Authenticity is a core value of communication – communicate with members how you would talk to them in a face-to-face meeting. Fake communication does not work well on LinkedIn.

- Customize your communication – often, people attempt to save time by sending a generic message with perhaps the name filled in with a mail-merge function. LinkedIn members do not react well to generic communication, and it is easy to tell if a member has spent the time to customize their communication.
- Be careful providing introductions to your network or colleagues to people you don't know well. Some members may ask for introductions to other members to assist in the sales process. The introductions act as a referral, making it easier for the salesperson to book a sales appointment.
- Respond quickly – if you take LinkedIn seriously for networking and connecting, treat your LinkedIn messages like your email inbox and respond to messages promptly with polite language.
- Edit yourself – since LinkedIn is a professional networking tool, you need to assume that current clients and prospective employers could be checking your messages and posts. Always be positive, use proper spelling and grammar, and maintain a professional, friendly tone.
- Be well-mannered – the purpose of LinkedIn is to build business relationships; therefore, make sure to say *please* and *thank you* between your correspondences.
- Professional writing uses a formal tone and is often used in the workplace to communicate with colleagues – slang terms are discouraged, and industry

jargon is often used as the audience is familiar with the terms.

- Professional writing is used to educate prospects in the lead generation process with high-quality content.

Summary of Key Points

- A professional must be an expert in their specialist field and always act in their client's interests.
- LinkedIn expects professional communication. Professional writing utilizes a formal style commonly used in the business environment.
- LinkedIn requires members to avoid being salesy, pushy, generic, or annoying. Standard cold marketing communication is not considered acceptable on the LinkedIn platform, and LinkedIn will restrict the account if such behavior is reported or detected.

The ancient Greeks regarded *love at first sight* as human madness expressed with wild passion. Cupid would fire 'love arrows,' and uncontrollable madness would ensue the subject. However, Plato presented a more sophisticated view; individual men and women existed as searching halves, craving to find their mate that would make them whole. Fusion unleashed uncontrollable energy.

Research has shown some scientific basis for *love at first sight.* There are two interesting findings in the vast sea of research and literature. First, scientists studied how long it takes a person to determine – or score – the physical attractiveness of another person. On average, it takes less than 0.2 seconds to do so, and the scores are quite consistent. This finding suggests that physical attractiveness is important and that it is related to facial structure. We tend to like people with symmetrical faces; it is as shallow as that.

The second finding is more interesting; the first few minutes of conversation (not the first impression) is a remarkably strong predictor of a future relationship. It is a strong predictor of how much the two people have in common and whether they *like* each other.

"Alicia, who is your worst salesperson?" I asked.

"Tim," Alicia replied.

"How far is he from making the budget?

"Tim is at about 50% of target, and we are about to have a discussion with him."

"Before you do that, can I have him for three months as my trainee?" I asked Alicia.

"Do you want the trial to fail?"

"No, what is the chance of Tim getting his target in the next quarter?"

"Zero," Alicia says instantly.

"So, if I work with him and he reaches the target, would you say the new program is working?"

"Yes," Alicia said with reluctance.

"Ok, when can I start?"

"Monday."

Perhaps Tim was a bridge too far. Sometimes I do that: get myself into trouble. I was excited as it was tremendous fun to try the impossible.

CHAPTER 10

Targeted Strategies

Technological progress promised magical productivity gains and free time for the tired worker. Instead, for many people in senior work roles, ubiquitous wireless internet and mobile devices have increased the volume and speed of work. Technology providers universally sold mobility as freedom. The tethered workplace was portrayed as stifling while working next to the pool was idyllic freedom. Ironically, the past tethered work practices enforced a level of freedom by limiting working hours to office hours. Time at home was free time that could be spent in refreshing, meaningful endeavors like family time. Mobile devices enabled work anywhere, resulting in voluntary slavery, not freedom. Work was no longer limited to weekdays. Mobility allows people to work every day and every awake hour. Consequently, stress and mental health issues spiraled out of control.

Walking my dog, Milly, in the local, national park released me from the draining daily grind. Thankfully, mobile coverage in the national park was limited, and Milly was not interested in a brisk walk.

Milly, a bouncing beige puppy cavoodle, was a much-loved birthday present for my 11-year-old daughter Melanie. As a young child, when your birthday is on the 26th of December, you may feel that life has cheated you out of half of your rightful quota of presents. The day before your birthday is Christmas Day, and Christmas presents often also serve as birthday presents. Melanie's 10th birthday destroyed this myth. The birthday present, Milly introduced herself by jumping on Melanie's lap and licking her face. The bond was immediate. Melanie never asked for nor wanted another birthday present.

As the sun was setting, I wondered what it would be like to have a simple life. What would I change? It was late Saturday afternoon, and I wanted to arrive home from our walk before the rain. Almost 300 yards from home, my iPhone started bleating as the signal strength came back to life.

I said, "Hello, Daniel."

Daniel Forbes was the most talented marketing professional I had met in my thirty-year career. He possessed a magical touch that generated crowds—an inexplicable skill derived from experience, not education. Daniel didn't understand what he was doing; he just produced results where other people failed.

Daniel's innate marketing ability to consistently generate large crowd attendance to events is perhaps the most sought-after treasure, yet his business was dangerously close to oblivion. Perhaps creative excellence struggles to co-exist with order and process. Why does the chosen one fail at the simple and excel at the impossible? Bizarre! Daniel's marketing understanding needed to be married with the systematic ways of business, and here is where I stepped in.

I asked, "Have you started implementing the job control software we discussed?" I took a deep breath at the question to calm myself because I already knew the answer.

"Not yet; I was too busy during the week."

I decided to push gently, "Daniel, what do you think will happen if you don't implement the job control software?"

"I know, but I have other things I also need to do."

I decided to divert and leave the confrontation until later "Have you thought of another great idea?"

I let Daniel talk uninterrupted for 35 minutes.

Sensing the appropriate time, "Daniel, I think that is a great idea. How do we start testing the idea on Monday?".

After Daniel hesitated, it allowed me to take the next small step. "You mentioned that not one of your staff members can sell like you. Why are you so good? What is the one thing that you do that is different?"

Daniel answered, "I hate wasting my time, so I always make sure I target the right person."

The Fill-the-Pipe Program

Lecture 10: Targeted Lead Generation Strategies

"Focus on identifying your target audience, communicating an authentic message that they want and need and project yourself as an "expert" within your niche."

Kim Garst

Broadcast lead generation strategies (discussed in the following lecture) are appropriate for businesses that sell low-ticket price items with a total annum spend of less than $5,000. Over the $5,000 annual spend threshold, targeted lead generation strategies become effective, and often a combination of both targeted and broadcast strategies will deliver the best results.

Targeting With Sales Navigator

- Sales and marketing professionals should consider subscribing to Sales Navigator (LinkedIn Premium) to access comprehensive, dynamic, real-time market information. Sales Navigator allows rapid target list creation based on the ideal prospect criteria.
- Lead generation campaigns can be implemented without the cost of a Sales Navigator subscription; however, it becomes a more complicated process.

The Targeted Approach

- Involves a tailored process that delivers individual personalized communication to each prospect, one at a time. The 5-step process includes:
  - Target
    - Using the criteria for your ideal customer profile, create the target prospect list with Sales Navigator.
  - Connect
    - Send personalized connection requests to the target list
  - Educate
    - Provide high-quality content
  - Nurture
    - Continue to build trust and credibility
  - Reach Out
    - At the right time, reach out to initiate telephone contact.

Optimizing the Targeted Approach

- The factors that can increase the response rate above 1% are:
    o Personalization and relevancy
    o Build trust
    o Engagement
    o Captivation
- The graph below shows typical results of what can be achieved with a well-executed campaign.

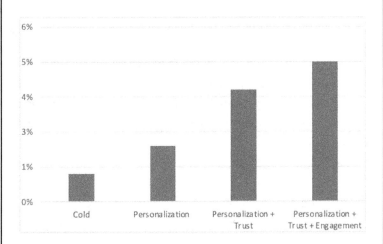

Personalization

- Personalization requires the user to view the target profile and create a tailored message relevant to the target member. It needs to highlight something that is in common between the two members.
- Many regard personalization as the key factor in improving marketing response rates, and

research shows that LinkedIn members now expect personalization.

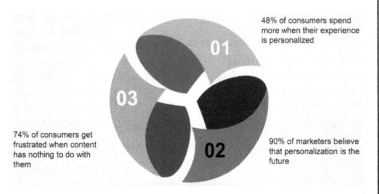

48% of consumers spend more when their experience is personalized

74% of consumers get frustrated when content has nothing to do with them

90% of marketers believe that personalization is the future

- Personalizing messages shows that you care enough to mention a person by name or cite their specific challenges; it can also set you apart from the dozens of other sales messages the prospect will be receiving every day.
- Personalization is more than a mail merge of the member's name. The sender needs to understand the target profile and communicate something relevant and exciting. It is the opposite of mass marketing, where the message is the same.
- Messaging members to ask permission for some information tends to be an effective way to start a conversation.
- Make sure that you show your interest in getting to know the target person and the company rather than immediately going into the sales pitch.
- Traditional cold marketing techniques are considered pushy and annoying in the LinkedIn community.

- Ensure that you demonstrate your knowledge and expertise by using the correct industry language. Jargon builds trust and rapport, showing that you may be a valuable resource in your specialty area.
- Maintain an attitude of professional helpfulness rather than salesmanship.
- Social selling aims to build relationships and trust over time rather than leveraging a quick sale.
- The objective of the sequence of messages is to earn the prospect's trust and book a brief phone call. The next step is to schedule a brief face-to-face or zoom meeting to start the buying process.

Accepted Personalized Connection Requests

- An event occurs when a personalized connection request is accepted; this is when the connection is no longer a cold prospect. It is now *warmer* since the recipient has viewed the sender's profile and decided that a relevancy threshold has been exceeded.
- After a member exceeds more than 9,000 personalized connections, a structured follow-up approach can deliver a continuous stream of warm leads.
    - o Each day, send 100 direct follow-up messages
    - o The result will be two or more warm leads per day
    - o After three months, the list of connections will be exhausted, and you can start from the top again.

- The graph above shows that personalization combined with trust-building strategies will outperform solely relying on personalization campaigns.

Build Trust

- Prospects are unlikely to respond to an approach if trust has not been built first.
- The response rate will be meager if the seller establishes a connection and pitches straight away.
- The seller needs to establish trust and credibility first.
- A high-quality content strategy is the most common way to build this relationship.
- Sellers need to establish themselves as an expert in the field through high-quality content.

Building a Trust Strategy With High-Quality Content

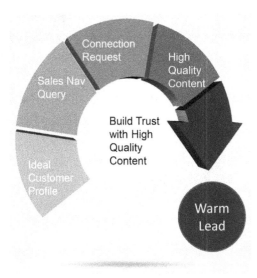

Trust Message Sequence

- Send a sequence of 3 or 4 high-quality articles, reports, or blogs
- The information needs to be:
  - Interesting
  - Educational
  - Useful
  - Practical
- In summary, the information needs to **add value.**

What happens?

- If the prospect has a need (business requirement) at the time of the conversation?
  - The prospect will contact the seller as one of the three vendors to evaluate before making a purchase decision.
- If the seller reaches out at the right time, a much more positive response will occur.

Engagement

- Engagement marketing is a marketing strategy that directly engages customers and invites them to participate in the brand experience.
- In LinkedIn marketing, you can view engagement as an extension of personalization.
- The seller can ask a question and start to engage in a conversation.

- It works better if the seller starts engagement after some trust has been established.

Build Trust & Engagement

Send High Quality Content

Ask a Relevant Question

Send Connection Request

Build Trust with Content & Engagement

Sales Nav Query

Ideal Customer

Warm Lead

Example

- Personalized Engagement Message
  - *"You mentioned in your profile that you have a passion for helping transform businesses with internet technology. The latest trend in the US is to use Machine Learning. If that is of interest, I can send you a good review article on the topic."*

Captivation

- Developing a great marketing strategy that excites and captivates the target market is difficult.
- Some classic examples include:
  - De Beers
    - "Diamonds Are Forever"
    - Launched in 1947 and is still in use. The slogan inspires consumers to view diamonds as a special timeless asset that deserves a price premium.
  - Nike
    - "Just Do It"
    - Nike embraced the slogan in 1988 while the company was in financial difficulties.
    - The slogan inspires consumers with a feeling of fearless adventure and encourages them to strive for their goals.
    - The success of this slogan is regarded as a crucial part of Nike's success
- Captivation strategies can be very effective as they attempt to carve out a space in the consumer's psyche. The most successful advertising campaigns manage to tie the products being sold to a meaningful catchy slogan.

- The process flow is shown below:

Captivation Offer

- An example of a captivation strategy that generated a strong result is an IT business process company that worked in the not-for-profit (NFT) industry. We created an NFP community hub that provided a forum for members to help each other, and we offered free membership. The positive response rate exceeded 20%. We had to reduce the number of messages sent each day by 90% as the response was overwhelming.

Summary of Key Points

- Sellers with a product or service that generates over the $5,000 annual spend threshold should consider a targeted lead generation strategy.
- Broadcast lead generation strategies (discussed in the following lecture) are appropriate for businesses that sell low-ticket price items with a total annum spend of less than $5,000.
- Targeted strategies focus on the ideal customer profile and create a personalized communication campaign that builds trust before reaching out with the sales pitch.

Psychology is the science that investigates human emotions, thoughts, and behavior. Science is supposed to be reliable, immutable, and provide answers. But human behavior seems unpredictable. How can you call psychology a science if it can't predict human behavior?

It was not until 1900 that William Stern resolved this vexed question, discovering differential psychology, the field that studies the individual difference in cognitive processes and behavior. Hence, a taxonomy of individual differences developed, and psychology regained respectability with predictable results inside nicely named groups.

The thought occurred to me that maybe Daniel was like Rain Man in the 1988 comedy-drama film directed by Barry Levinson. In 1887, Dr. Langdon Down devised the term *idiot savant*; it labels a person with an extraordinary memory yet poor reasoning. Daniel possessed high intelligence and tremendous creativity but poor commonsense and ordinary life skills. If I was right, then I knew how to help Daniel start implementing his ideas.

Eventually, a Master Coach develops enough skills to be guided by feeling, not thinking. Great coaches are rarely great initially; it takes time to learn the craft. After a decade, coaching becomes like changing the gears on a manual car. The spare cognitive capacity allows the coach to think about his thinking process (meta-cognition) while attentively mulling important conversational nuances with the client. Please do not misunderstand; meta-cognition is not crude multitasking. The Master Coach can work in two parallel universes, neglecting neither. The breakthroughs occur in the intersections where insight in one domain is applied to the other domain.

I was bursting with excitement. The Rain Man insight, if correct, was the key to understanding how to work effectively with Daniel. Perhaps today, mobile technology late Saturday afternoon reduced my stress for a change, and I arrived home before the rain.

CHAPTER 11

Broadcast Strategies

Tyler MacDonald was the most talented marketing professional I had ever met until I encountered Daniel Forbes. Tyler was Daniel's reverse doppelganger. Blessed with a penchant for amazingly creative marketing strategy grounded in solid marketing theory, Tyler managed to grow a business from nothing to $125m per annum revenue in less than 18 months, but again oblivion was approaching fast. Had the two gentlemen worked together, the team would have been unstoppable. However, they were in different states, blossomed in completely different industries, and played the game at other times.

Tyler was a lovable pirate in the mold of Captain Jack Sparrow from the Pirates of the Caribbean film. The extravert's extravert, Tyler liked everyone, and he loved to chat – mostly about himself or his latest genius marketing idea. And I don't use the word *genius* lightly. As a seasoned management consultant, I was exposed to strategy in many forms, including the business strategy formulation for two different fortune 50 US corporations. Appreciating the beauty of an intelligent business strategy, I was rarely impressed, yet Tyler managed to mesmerize me.

Lunches with Tyler were delightful. Pepper steak medium rare, chips, and beer provided sustenance, and Tyler was the entertainment. The ideas were brilliant, sometimes even genius, but the implementation was always tragic. Even if Tyler implemented only 5% of his ideas, the business would have grown to epic proportions.

Implementing a mediocre strategy is better than not implementing a genius one. Once you have developed a basic marketing strategy (and it does not have to be great), you need to implement and then learn from the outcomes; rarely does the first idea become a great strategy. Learning occurs when the information is broadcasted to a sample of prospects and feedback is provided.

The Fill-the-Pipe Program

Lecture 11: Broadcast Strategies

"Storytelling is the most powerful way to put ideas into the world today."

Robert McKee

Social media enables people to connect, communicate and share information to build communities around shared values and common interests. Occasionally, content can spread virally. Viral content occurs when the content captures the imagination of members and is shared with millions of other members. Marketers dream of leveraging social media to generate massive brand awareness and interest through viral marketing campaigns.

Social networking sites facilitate viral content

- Viral marketing is when members proactively send content to other members with a *word-of-mouth* recommendation.
- Social networking sites provide software tools to build virtual communities that allow customers to express their opinions online. It enables members and businesses to interact and build virtual relationships online. Companies can communicate with customers directly more personally than through traditional marketing methods.
- Marketers can use direct customer feedback instead of costly market research.
- Customer opinions and feedback can act as powerful *word-of-mouth* marketing tools that also has the potential to go viral.

Viral Marketing

- Viral marketing is a powerful method of building brand recognition. Marketers attempt to encourage their customers and prospects to share their content on social media platforms.
- The potential to rapidly change purchasing decisions of large customer networks is called an influence network. Leveraging an influencer's network with a successful campaign can rapidly grow sales revenue with minimal costs.
- For example, when Cristiano Ronaldo, the famous soccer player, endorses products, he can positively

influence more than 40 million followers to consider product purchases.

- Using influencers can be an efficient and cost-effective method to market. For example, The Indian Prime Minister Narendra Modi has more than 40 million followers. Modi bypassed traditional media to reach out to young voters, just as President Trump successfully exploited Twitter to galvanize Republican support in the US 2016 election.

Viral Content

- Content can 'go viral' because social media platforms encourage the creation of viral content by providing convenient and straightforward functional, re-share content. For example, Twitter has the 'retweet' button, and Facebook uses the 'share' option.
- Marketers attempt to employ viral marketing campaigns to:
  - o Gain access to vast target audiences
  - o Dramatically reduce the cost compared to traditional advertising campaigns

The Nike #MakeItCount Campaign Increased Profit by Almost 20%

- The 2012 Nike #MakeItCount campaign is an example of a viral marketing campaign.
- Launched in 2012, Neistat and Joseph created a YouTube video chronicling their 34,000 miles journey to visit 16 cities in 13 countries. Using the

#MakeItCount hashtag. A hashtag is a keyword or phrase that starts with the hash symbol, "#." It enables easy cross-referencing of content on social media.

- The video was shared by millions of people on Twitter and Instagram. The campaign went viral, and Nike increased its profit by almost 20% during the campaign.

Posts That Get Shared More Often

- Posts that are shared on Linkedin tend to do the following:
  - Evoke positive emotion
  - Are controversial or shock the audience
  - Are amusing or visually pleasing
  - Discuss how to build communities

Algorithms to Help Build Viral Content

- Many social media platforms, not including LinkedIn, provide specific functionality that increases the probability of member content going viral.
- The TikTok social media platform has over 1.5 billion users, and the members are mainly children and teenagers. TikTok developed simple functionality with a wide range of special effects and fun daily challenges. The functionality encourages user creativity with special effects, and users tend to create more exciting content, which is then more likely to be shared.

Viral Videos

- Most viral videos contain an element of humor. Viral videos tend to be in one or more of these categories:
  - Humorous
  - Accidental
  - Promotional
  - Charity
  - Artistic
  - Political

Examples of Viral Videos

Some examples of viral videos include:

- 1. Barack Obama's *'Yes We Can'* campaign created a YouTube video
- 2. First Kiss Youtube video created by Tatia Pilieva
- 3. Ice Bucket challenge

Posting Content on Linkedin

- It is challenging to create great content regularly. Consider outsourcing the role to a professional web content creator.
- Remember that the goal is to build brand awareness, increase engagement and promote expertise in the chosen field.
- Promote expertise by providing:
  - Valuable tips
  - Relevant articles

- o Industry trends
- o Case Studies
- o Success Stories
- Share Best Practices
  - o Help the target audience solve part of their problem
  - o Products and services can form part of the solution
  - o Educate, do not sell. Use a problem-solution structure in the communication. The problem needs to match the business challenge, and it should be based on substance and not be promotional
- Share Milestones
  - o Adding reviews and testimonials from customer engagements can build brand credibility.
- 'Share the work' approach.
  - o Explaining the solution builds trust and credibility.

How to Increase Engagement on Posts

- Pictures, not text.
- Posts containing images that capture attention, engaging videos, slideshows, and polls perform better than text-only posts.
- Make sure that you do not
  - o use too many hashtags,
  - o share other people's posts, or
  - o use external links without permission.

- You also want to add spaces between lines to decrease text-heavy and facilitate a pleasant reading experience.
- Keep the language professional and non-technical.
- Write in short sentences and paragraphs.
- Adding emojis tends to increase the engagement of posts as the emojis can clarify the tone of content and express emotion.
- Use primary colors on the images to capture attention.

Frequency

- The biggest mistake sellers make posting good content and stopping because they are swamped with work and get too busy. The start/stop activity damages the brand because it suggests that the seller is unreliable.
- It is essential to maintain the quality and frequency of posts. Ideally, the frequency of posts should be once or twice a week.
- Quality is more important than quantity, so don't post just for posting.
- The next step is to start engaging with the audience. Start liking and commenting on other posts in your community, and often members will return the favor.

Summary of Key Points

- Social media enables people to connect, communicate and share information to build communities around shared interests.
- Occasionally content can spread virally, and this occurs when the content captures the imagination of members and is shared with millions of other members.
- Viral marketing campaigns have the potential to generate massive brand awareness and brand equity.

The Pirates of the Caribbean movie franchise was tremendously successful financially. It grossed more than $4.5 billion and placed in the top 15 highest-grossing film series. Johnny Depp's inspired performance as Captain Jack Sparrow was pivotal to the success.

The character of Jack Sparrow emerged from the amalgamation of the musician Keith Richards and the cartoon character Pepé Le Pew. Lurking from one crisis to the next, Jack Sparrow survives using his mystic intelligence and skillful negotiation. Unfortunately, Johnny Depp, the actor who plays Jack Sparrow, was not endowed with the same powers. Depp earned more than $300m from the Pirates of the Caribbean films yet managed to accumulate precious little apart from owing the government $100 million in unpaid taxes.

Marketing is taught in business schools as a rigorous discipline and a predictable science. Marketing does have some helpful theory, but when it submerges in the practical details of executing a real-life campaign, the mandate becomes A/B testing. The essence of the approach is trial and error testing. The polite explanation is that the predictable science of Marketing is a young emerging science requiring more research.

Art rather than science is what drives monstrous success. Social media may be the vehicle, but spectacular creativity drives viral campaigns. In 2014, Tatia Pilieva uploaded the legendary YouTube video called *First Kiss*. The video clip describes a fascinating social experiment where twenty strangers are split into pairs and asked to kiss for the first time. The video records their hesitation and experience. The clip went viral and has recorded over 150 million views. The video is a 3-minute masterpiece that demonstrates that viral campaigns do not need to be complex, it just needs to be exciting and creative. The YouTube URL is: https://www.youtube.com/watch?v=IpbDHxCV29A&t=1s

"Tyler, last week we discussed the importance of focusing and finishing one thing before starting something else. How did you go since our last meeting?" I asked

"I was flat out, but I have another idea," Tyler replied.

"I love hearing your ideas, but before we go down that rabbit hole.

Let's see if we can go back to last week's idea."

"I just don't have the time?"

Ignoring Tyler's excuse, I probed, "How many admin staff do you have?"

"Ten full-time and three part-time."

"Who is the manager?"

"Charlotte."

I suggested, trying a different approach, "Can you get Charlotte to do the simple bits and start the program this week? Does Charlotte have enough time?"

Tyler was emphatic, "Yes, I am sure she has plenty of time."

Every week we would go through the same ritual. The core expertise of the Master is 'behavior change,' but in this case, I lost the battle of helping Tyler implement his great ideas. Sad because the business had revenue greater than $125m, and if it had implemented even one of Tyler's ideas, it would have at least doubled. Ten years later, with many more miles on the speedo, I know what I should have done, and I will leave the answer for my next book.

Remember, no matter how creative or brilliant you are, nothing will happen if you don't implement.

CHAPTER 12

Accelerator Strategies

Sixteen thousand car accidents each year occur when drivers push the accelerator pedal instead of the brake in the US. A rare group of unfortunates causes accidents in the reverse direction. I belong to this group, and I almost killed myself (by accident) 20 years ago, and it was close.

The gas pedal controls fuel and air to the engine and is the 'accelerator.' It is the righthand side pedal on the car's floor. Press the pedal, and the vehicle accelerates. If you want to slow down, remove your foot from the gas and hit the brake pedal. It sounds simple, doesn't it?

After a long week at work, late Friday afternoon, I was driving on a flat, narrow, windy road on top of a mountain range: Easy terrain, no rain, and no traffic in the opposite direction. I was tired, but that is an excuse, as I could have stopped for a rest anytime. My foot was aching, so I was playing with different positions on the gas pedal. My foot slipped off the top of the gas pedal and crashed down on the brake. My brand-new Mercedes C200 was equipped with superbly efficient ABS brakes. The unsuspecting driver tailgating me was surprised. Today as I recount the story, my eyes are watering with laughter, but it wasn't funny at the time. Mr. Tradie's truck hit the side of my car at an angle, I spun out of control, and my car almost made a 2,000-foot drop. Mr. Tradie jumped out of his car, swearing uncontrollably like a mad man with turrets. He was definitely not concerned with my health. I suspect Mr. Tradie likes to partake in Friday afternoon drinks and was not pleased with the prospect of discussing with the local police.

By the time the police arrived, I had come to my senses, and I mostly repeated the same question:

"Why did you crash into the back of my car? You must have been going very, very fast."

The policeman did not believe that anyone would be silly enough to slam on the brakes for no reason, and Mr. Tradie was carted off for a drug test. Very funny indeed, but there were consequences; my whiplash for a few weeks, and I was without a car for a month.

Automation tools are abundant in daily life, accelerating the time to complete common tasks. The accelerator can also be dangerous if it is not used carefully in the appropriate manner. The chainsaw in the hands of an experienced tradesman does a week's work in a few hours. In the hands of a Mr. Bean, it could be ugly.

The Fill-the-Pipe Program

Lecture 12: Accelerator Strategies

"We become what we behold. We shape our tools, and thereafter our tools shape us."

Marshall McLuhan

Well-executed targeted lead generation strategies will typically deliver a positive response rate between 1-5%. The response rate depends heavily on the quality of the execution of each step. This lecture described an additive strategy that sits on top of the previous process and can boost the response rate to approximately 20%. Named *accelerator strategies* enable a bland sales and marketing process to deliver superior results.

The Shift from Passive to Proactive Campaigns

- Accelerator strategies are effective because they shift the marketing focus from passive to proactive campaigns based on high-quality personalized connections.
- The graph below shows the typical increase in performance.

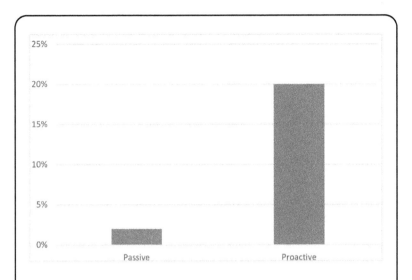

Proactive Strategies

- Several different proactive strategies can be employed. The two most common include:
  - Invitation to a Webinar
  - Telephone Call
- There are four different types of proactive follow-up calls:
  - Cold
  - Research
  - Referral, and
  - Research Referral
- Cold calls are not recommended, only warm calls. Remember, the calls should not be performed until after built trust with high-quality message sequences.
- The graph below shows the typical increase in performance with accelerator strategies.

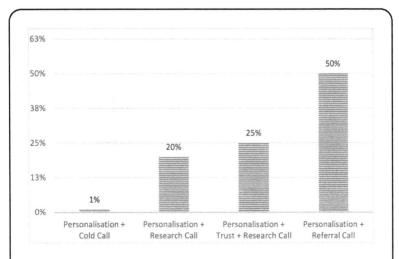

- The more the communication is specifically customized to the target industry and the target member, the better the response rate.
- A common mistake is to use accelerator strategies too early in the process. The accelerator strategies should only be invoked after trust has been established with the personalized, targeted strategies.

Research Calls

- The research call is a more effective version of the traditional cold call. There is a virtual relationship that the personalized connection has established; however, it is rarely strong enough to start the buying process.
- The Research Call attempts to bridge the relationship gap.
- An example research script is shown below:

Hi Chris,

{Introduction}

My name is Richard from ABC.

How are you today?

Do you have 5 minutes for a brief chat now, or should I call back?

NO

OK, what is a good time to call you?

YES

Thanks

We are specialists in social proof systems.

{Discuss an issue in the industry}

I have been doing some research on your company.

I read your annual report on your website, and it seems that increasing your Online sales is a high strategic priority.

Is that still The case?

YES

OK

We increase your Online Sales by 10-20% using new social Proof systems software technology.

We have a few clients in your industry, and our solution is working well for them.

It doesn't work for everyone, so we need to chat to see if it would work for your business.

I don't want to waste your time now.

{Ask for something small – a brief call or a coffee}

Do you have time for a brief 15-minute call next week to discuss your business?

What day/time would suit you next week?

- Note that there will still be up to 50% of target members that are annoyed to receive the research call. A LinkedIn direct message warning the target of the impending call helps alleviate much of the negativity.
- Approximately 50% of the recipients will accept the call, and about 20% of the calls will have a positive response. If the caller does not reach these metrics, then often, there is something wrong in the delivery of the call.

Research Referral Calls

- Referral calls are the most effective calls. The positive response rate is typically over 50%.
- An example research referral script is shown below:

Hi {first name},

{Introduction}

My name is Adrian from DEF.

How are you today?

Do you have 5 minutes for a brief chat now, or should I call back?

NO

OK, what is a good time to call you?

YES

{Start with the name of the referrer}

{referral name} suggested that I give you a call.

{Discuss an issue in the industry}

I understand that your business uses a crypto-currency, and I wanted to mention that crypto-currencies are a favorite for Cyber hackers. My expertise is protecting against Cyber-attacks in your industry.

{Ask for something small – a brief call or a coffee}

Do you have time for a brief 15-minute call next week to discuss your Cyber protection?

What day/time would suit you next week?

Preparation Time

- Preparation time is the key to effective calling. The graph below shows that the more preparation before the call, the better the results.

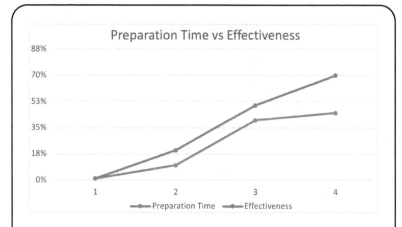

- The more the communication is specifically customized to the target industry and the target member, the better the response rate.

Daily Routine

- Most salespeople do not enjoy calling and procrastinate when faced with a task. A standard solution is to reserve the first 90 minutes every morning and dedicate this time to calling new prospects. That may be between 9 am – 10.30 am every workday. Strict discipline is required to enforce the routine.

Summary of Key Points

- Well-executed targeted lead generation strategies will typically deliver a positive response rate between 1-5%. The response rate depends heavily on the quality of the execution of each step.

- Accelerator strategies are an additive strategy that sits on top of the targeted lead generation approach and can boost the response rate to approximately 20%.
- Accelerator strategies enable a bland sales and marketing process to deliver superior results.

Many years later, my daughter turned 21, and for her birthday, I bought her a new Mazda 2 car. Mazda developed a unique organ-type accelerator pedal by looking at the website specs. To make the vehicle idiot-proof (Chris proof), the driver puts their right foot on a particular position on the floor (not the top). It is designed to make the accelerator pedal easier to control because the heel is stabilized – ergonomic plus design. Mazda claims that the driver's foot naturally rests to reduce driving fatigue and accidents. Yes, I agree.

As time passes, accelerator tools become more sophisticated, solve more problems and prevent more cases of human error. As the tools become smarter, there is a natural tendency for the human user to become complacent. Better tools do not mean that the user can abdicate the responsibility of careful thought and appropriate planning. Accelerator strategies are compelling, but be careful.

CHAPTER 13

Over Delivery

Reflecting on my 35-year selling and delivering consulting career, I identified three factors that made a difference. Of course, there is the list of usual suspects: persistence, dedication, positive mental attitude, et cetera, and you do need all of that, but I call these factors *basic hygiene*. In tennis, you must be able to hit the ball back over the net to be in the game. That is the minimum, but you will never win a match if that is all you can do. There are thousands of books that discuss basic hygiene, and many of them are very good; however, this chapter is not about hygiene; it is about how to *win* the match.

1. The Hand of God

Christians call it the *Hand of God*, nonbelievers call it luck, romantics call it destiny, and skeptics call it a random event. Terminology is not important to me; I merely grabbed the opportunity when it appeared.

Steven Bradbury is an Olympic Champion touched by the Hand of God twice.

Bradbury was the second oldest and one of the slowest competitors in the Salt Lake City 2002 Winter Olympics. Reaching the Olympic final was a forlorn hope. In the semifinals, only the first two skaters advance to the finals. As expected, the aging Bradbury was in last place. The titans Dong-sung, Jiajun, and Turcotte were involved in a bitter struggle when a split-second micro-error swept the three campaigners onto the ice in a cacophony of sprawling arms and legs. Crash! Bradbury won the semifinal.

Bradbury was in fifth place with less than 100m to the finish in the final, a tremendous effort from the old lion. The family was already proud, but the race was not yet over. The gold medal struggle is the most intense in the last 100 yards. The four young champions: Ohno, Ahn Hyun-Soo, Li, and Turcotte, were fighting with all their strength for gold, yet glory vanished in a split second. In a dramatic event, the dreams of all four competitors were destroyed 50 yards before the finish line. Bradbury was far enough behind to avoid the carnage and snatch the gold. The accidental champion was the first person from the southern hemisphere to win a Winter Olympic gold medal.

The world media had a new darling, and in the swarm of interviews that followed, Bradbury claimed that his strategy was deliberate. Understanding his limitations as the second-oldest skater, he knew he would never be able to compete on raw speed; he hoped – not planned – for an opportunistic win.

In an interview, Bradbury said, "I was the oldest bloke on the field, and I knew that. Skating four races back-to-back, I wouldn't have any petrol left in the tank. So, there was no point in getting there and mixing it up because I would be in last place anyway. So, I might as well stay out of the way and be in last place and hope that some people get tangled up."

I believe him.

The media loved the story of an accidental champion. The true story didn't need an angle to make it more interesting. Bradbury handled the disrespectful questions well. Did he think that he deserved the gold medal? The answer was profound.

Bradbury said, "Obviously, I wasn't the fastest skater. I don't think I'll take the medal as the minute-and-a-half of the race I won; I'll take it as the last decade of the hard slog I put in."

My definition of *luck* is the appearance of a rare opportunity you did not deserve. Bradbury is not in that category; he definitely earned the medal.

My career was defined by three major reverse Bradbury moments, and they forged the overriding philosophy of the over-delivery approach. It is the final and most crucial piece of the puzzle.

Before my twenty-second birthday, I graduated from University with an Honors degree in computer science, majoring in youthful arrogance. The joy of youth is that you don't know what you don't know, and you think that you can conquer the world. My naivety and arrogance were tempered with hard work and excellent technical knowledge. Technically, I was strong at IT, and my timing was perfect. I took the opportunity presented before me because I didn't think about the risk. I said to myself, *'How hard can this be?'*

I took a job with a small IT business straight out of university. The owner, Jules Moffat, was short and well-fed. He was a smoker and was excited about getting married for the fourth time to a beautiful, young fiancé. A week before the wedding, Jules was hit by a massive heart attack, and he died in the best way: with a smile on his face.

The 1998 movie, *Sliding Doors*, is a poignant rom-com written and directed by Peter Howitt.

Gwyneth Paltrow leads a strong cast, including John Hannah and Jeanne Tripplehorn. The plot charts the development of two parallel stories that depend on a random event – catching a train. Life consequences depend on catching or not catching the train, thus the title *Sliding Doors* of the train. It is a clever metaphor for life as trains take passengers on a journey. The film explores the fascinating question, *Can a small decision or random event totally change the entire outcome of your life?* It certainly can.

My *Sliding Doors* moment occurred a week after John passed. The customers approached me directly and invited me to continue their work. For me, it was an easy decision, and I said, "Yes." Of course, the reason was simple – *how hard can this be?*

After Jules tripped and fell on the ice rink, I stepped up, received my gold medal, and began my decade of hard work.

Whether you believe in the Hand of God or luck is not material in this quest, life presents opportunities to everyone continuously. It is up to you to have the courage (or naivety) to take the opportunity. The worst that can happen is that you fail, which is often good. Failure forces you to learn, but success is a poor teacher.

2. The Hard Easy Road

It is not an exaggeration to say that the sales trainer, Gerald, changed my life. Chris, the young Master, was young but not yet a master. He was technically proficient but lacking in every other skill. Life travels with no empathy; the lessons roll forward whether you are ready or not. Learning occurs with an open personality when no one else is to blame – in other words, rarely.

Gerald's passion for sales training was infectious, and the skills required were noted. Gerald loved to speak in riddles and quotes. Perhaps, he liked other people's sayings better than his own. For Gerald, sales training was a theatrical performance; it allowed him to show off his deep knowledge without the pressure of exceeding a sales budget. All care and no responsibility, a perfect role for the guru. The career choice would have been perfect, except the only challenge for Gerald was volume. Gerald's sales training happened once every few months, which is not enough to feed the family.

Gerald's favorite saying was, "The hard easy road or the easy hard road." I do not know the creator's origin, but I know it would not have been my friend Gerald. Initially, the meaning may somewhat be opaque. The intention is to distinguish whether to do something correctly or take the shortcut. The consequence is that the shortcut is likely to be more difficult as the solution may not be complete.

I tend to pick the hard easy road because shortcuts will always take longer.

3. Fight like a bulldog to keep Tier-1s

Steven Covey wrote the mega-bestseller *The 7 Habits of Highly Effective People*. The book is elaborate in its messaging for its readers, which you would expect from a book that sold more than 25 million copies worldwide. The habits mentioned are common-sensical and very useful indeed.

As a Covey pilgrim, I like *to begin with the end in sight*. In other words, you need to decide what you want to achieve and clearly understand the goal, Sage's advice that applies universally.

The goal of our program is to find 10 to 20 tier-1 clients who continuously spend every month. The book has described how to acquire these tier-1 customers as the effort to win over this tier is significant, and the cost is high. Therefore, once you have a tier-1 customer, you should try and hold onto them for as long as possible. How do you do that? The answer is simple.

Merely *over-deliver* to the tier-1 customers; the strategy optimizes revenue and profit.

The Fill-the-Pipe Program

Lecture 13: Over Delivery

"Customer satisfaction is worthless. Customer loyalty is priceless."

Jeffrey Gitomer

The cost of new customer acquisition is high compared to servicing existing customers. New customer acquisition costs are often more than the gross profit derived from recent customer purchases in the first 6 or 12 months. Therefore, if the business expends its effort to create new customers, it should develop customer retention and repurchase system to maximize the return. The simplest and most powerful strategy to achieve customer longevity is to understand the lifetime value of the tier-1 customer and make sure that the business over-delivers to your tier-1 customer in the first 6-12 months.

Customer Retention & Repurchase

- Customer retention systems are processes that encourage customers to stay loyal to the business and continue to purchase products and services.

- For example, a coffee shop may issue a loyalty card that enables the customer to get one free coffee after purchasing ten coffees.
- A rule of thumb is:
  - Increasing retention rates by 5% can increase revenue by 20% and profit by 10%.
- The importance of customer retention and repurchase systems can change the structure of a whole industry. The software industry moved from a one-off capital purchase revenue model to the Software-as-a-Service (SaaS) subscription-based revenue model over the last 20 years.
- Research by BMC found that the SaaS market is currently growing by 18% each year, and by the end of 2022, over 95% of businesses will be using one or more SaaS solutions.
- Nearly 78% of US small businesses have already invested in at least one SaaS solution.

Customer Retention Strategies

- Great customer experiences – A common customer retention strategy is to provide consistently excellent customer experiences. That could include:
  - Fast support
  - Regular customer meetings
  - Friendly and responsive staff
- A better customer retention strategy than *great customer experiences* focuses on building strong business relationships and delivering outstanding value.

- The core principle is to:
    - Put the customer first and continually add real value to the customer
- Simple hygiene behaviors are essential
    - **Show genuine interest**: Be proactive and ask for feedback
    - **Fast and responsive**: Makes sure salespeople return calls and answer questions promptly.
    - **Be engaging**: Ask customers questions about themselves.
    - **Anticipate**: As the customer relationship develops, understanding the customer requirements should also deepen.
    - **Follow up**: Thank you notes, and phone calls help customers feel appreciated.
- Be Professional
    - Be courteous (say please and thank you)
    - Dress appropriately for the role
    - Avoid the three controversial topics:
        - Religion
        - Politics
        - Sex
- Show Reliability and Integrity
    - Customers trust businesses and individuals when they show reliability and integrity. Reliability means that the customer can expect a consistent experience when dealing with the company.

Monitoring Customer Retention Metrics

- Three important customer retention metrics should be monitored:
  o Customer Retention Rate
  o Churn Rate
  o Lifetime Customer Value
- The customer retention rate is the percentage of customers that stay loyal to the business over a specific period.
- The churn rate (attrition rate) is the number of customers leaving a business over a defined period.
- Businesses that struggle with customer retention have a high churn rate. Low retention rates or churn rates are an early warning sign that the business may be headed for misfortune.
- The customer's lifetime value is the total revenue the customer spends with the business until they leave.

Over-Deliver to the Tier-1 New Customers

- The simplest and most powerful strategy to achieve tier-1 customer longevity is to understand the lifetime value of the tier-1 customer and make sure that the business over-delivers in the first 6-12 months.
- After 12 months of over-delivery, the business relationship will usually translate into a stable level of customer loyalty. Insulating the business against the most competitive threats.
- The two most important factors are:

o Build a strong business relationship with the customer

o Put the customer first and continually add real value to the customer

Summary of Key Points

- The cost of new customer acquisition is high compared to servicing existing customers. New customer acquisition costs are often more than the gross profit derived from the first 6 or 12 months of new customer purchases.
- The business should develop customer retention and repurchase system to maximize the return.

CHAPTER 14

Time to Start

The treasure is found, and the mystery is solved. Is that the end? No. Now the hard work begins.

The easiest and fastest way to implement the lead generation program is to hire a qualified coach or professional consultant familiar with the program to lead the project. The consultant can help tailor the system to your industry and business requirements. Alternatively, you can contact the author Chris Harasty by email at: chris@harasty.com.au.

For people who prefer the do-it-yourself approach, please take note. Coaching yourself is difficult, and it requires sustained effort and persistence for success. It is essential to develop a detailed plan and maintain consistent effort to overcome the inevitable obstacles faced in the journey ahead. The detailed scripts are included in the next section. Good luck in your journey, and don't hesitate to get in touch with us if you need help.

The Fill-the-Pipe Program

Lecture 14: The Scripts

"A bad system will beat a good person every time."

W. Edwards Deming

The renowned economist W. Edwards Deming championed the concept that processes and procedures are the foundation of good businesses. Deming said, "If you can't describe what you are doing as a process, you don't know what you're doing." The equivalent concept in the fill-the-pipe program is the detailed scripts – ignore them at your peril.

Connection Requests

- The typical generic connection request is the default message provided by LinkedIn:
  Hi George, I would like to add you to our professional network.
- The acceptance rate for a generic connection request tends to be about 10%.
- Personalized connection requests require time and effort from the user to view the target profile and create a relevant, customized message.

- The process flow is described in the diagram below:

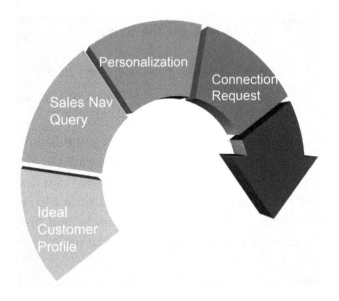

- Personalization requires the sender to review the target's LinkedIn profile and craft a message that is:
    - Based on specific information in the target profile
    - Relevant and interesting
    - Highlights something in common

- For example, the script below:

Hi {NAME},

I noticed that we both have an interest in Cyber Security, and we both studied IT at Washington University. It would be good to connect.

Regards

{YOUR NAME}

- Personalized connection requests have a much higher acceptance rate. The rate varies depending on the market and seniority of the target, and typically, the acceptance rate is between 40 – 50%.
- Below is an example of the typical acceptance rate for personalized connection requests:

ABC Company	13/09 Mon	14/09 Tue	15/09 Wed	16/09 Thu	17/09 Fri	Week Total
Connection Requests Sent	20	20	20	20	20	**100**
Connections Accepted	13	8	9	8	11	**49**
Percentage	**65%**	**40%**	**45%**	**40%**	**55%**	**49%**

Direct Messages

- Direct messages can only be sent to 1st-degree connections. The message needs to be written in a professional style and have the following characteristics:
  o Relevant
  o Interesting
  o Useful
  o Practical
  o Add value
- The process flow is described in the diagram below:

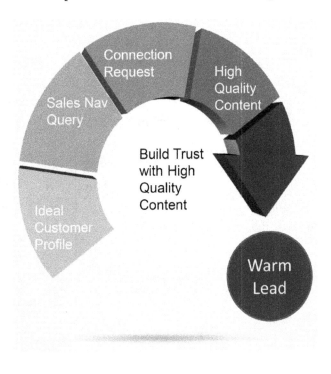

- The script is:

Hi {NAME},

Traditionally IAST tools have been plagued with the challenges of scalability and accuracy.

The article below describes how to solve these challenges.

www.yourwebsite/article01

If you'd like more information, we can have a brief chat next week.

What day/time suits you next week?

Regards,
Chris

The Cold Calling Script

- The anatomy of a cold calling script
  - 1. Open the conversation
  - 2. Interest grabbing statement
  - 3. Open-ended questions
  - 4. Close the call

Hi Joe,

My name is George. I am from Impressive Energy.

We save you money on your electricity bills.

We have a special 20% discount offer that expires at the end of the week.

How much money do you spend on your electricity bill per quarter?

Can you please send me an old bill so I can have a look and work out how much you will save?

Et cetera

The Research Call Script

- The anatomy of a research calling script
  - o 1. Introduction
  - o 2. Research
  - o 3. Pitch
  - o 4. Close the call

<Intro Section>

Hi Justin,

Les from Fast Printing calling.
How are you today?

{Let them answer – good etc.}

We connected on LinkedIn a few weeks ago.
Is now a good time for a brief 2-minute chat?

{Let them answer – most will say yes
If not, ask when to ring back.}

OK, what is a good time to call for a brief chat?

<Research Section>

Option 1 – Info from the LinkedIn Profile

Reading your LinkedIn profile, I noticed that you XXXXX.

Option 2 – Info from the website – annual report
I have read the annual report from your website, and it mentions that your two most important strategic priorities are:

1. XXXX
2. XXXX

Is that still the same, or has it changed?

Option 3 – Industry Research
I have been working in and researching your industry, and it seems that the two important priorities at the moment are:

1. XXXX
2. XXXX

Is that still the same for your organization?

{If the answer is NO – ask what the priorities are}
{If that the answer is YES}

<Short Pitch Section>

We have a good solution for XXXX, and it uses new software technology.
We have several happy clients using the solution.

It doesn't work for every business, and I don't want to waste your time now.

Do you have time for a brief 15min coffee next week or the week after to discuss if our solution would work for your business?

What day and time would suit you for a brief 15 min coffee?

What is your email address? And I will send you an invitation.

Thanks

The Referral Call Script

- The anatomy of a research calling script
  - o 1. Introduction
  - o 2. Name the referral source
  - o 3. Pitch
  - o 4. Close the call

Hi Joe,

My name is Chris Harasty. I am from Harasty Consulting.

George Smith recommended that I give you a call.

What we do is XYZ.

George has been using our service for a while, and he thinks it is excellent.

George suggested that I give you a call.

Is XYZ something that may interest you?

Our product does not work for everybody. We would need to have a brief discussion to see if it suits your organization.

Do you have time for a brief 15-minute coffee next week?

What day/time would suit you?

Summary of Key Points

- The renowned economist W. Edwards Deming said:
  - "A bad system will beat a good person every time," and
  - "If you can't describe what you are doing as a process, you don't know what you're doing."
- The equivalent concept in the fill-the-pipe program is the detailed scripts – ignore them at your peril.

www.ingramcontent.com/pod-product-compliance
Lightning Source LLC
Chambersburg PA
CBHW071129050326
40690CB00008B/1388